P9-DEK-956

GREAT BATTLES

An Imprint of Sterling Publishing
1166 Avenue of the Americas
New York, NY 10036

ISBN 978-1-4351-6997-5

For information about custom editions, special sales, and premium and corporate purchases, please contact Sterling Special Sales at 800-805-5489 or specialsales@sterlingpublishing.com.

Manufactured in Singapore

2 4 6 8 10 9 7 5 3 1

sterlingpublishing.com

GREAT BATTLES

LANDMARK EVENTS

PETER DARMAN

METRO BOOKS
New York

Contents

> “Mankind must put an end to war, or war will put an end to mankind.”
>
> —JOHN F. KENNEDY

Introduction

Human history has been shaped by conflict, from clashes between Egyptian pharaohs and Roman commanders, to modern warfare. This book allows you to dip in and out of history and discover more about the conflicts that helped to shape the modern world.

The first clear historical record for a clash of arms relates to the Battle of Megiddo, fought in the 15th century BCE between King Thutmose III of Egypt and the king of the Syrian city of Kadesh. Although battles and skirmishes took place before this, the lack of records leaves us with lots of questions. Even the precise date of Megiddo is still shrouded in mystery, with historians dating the battle to 1457, 1479, or 1482 BCE. For this reason, Megiddo and other ancient battles have been ommitted from this book.

“Never in the field of human conflict was so much owed by so many to so few.”

—WINSTON CHURCHILL

Many of the battles fought and won by history's great commanders are included in the book, not only for the leadership skills of the leader in question, but because they often changed the course of history. For example, Alexander the Great's victory at Gaugamela in 331 BCE brought about the

▶ Troops of the 55th New York Regiment at Fort Gaines, near Tenley, D.C., during the American Civil War.

collapse of the Persian Empire and made him master of Asia. Similarly, Admiral Nelson's victory at Trafalgar in 1805, during the Napoleonic Wars, made the British Royal Navy mistress of the oceans and accelerated the growth of the British Empire.

Another great commander featured in this book is Napoleon Bonaparte. His victory at Austerlitz in 1805 brought most of Europe under his control. Napoleon changed the way war was waged, specifically, in the realm of strategy.

After his defeat at Waterloo in 1815, battles grew in scale, duration, and intensity, with corresponding loss of life. Advances in technology, specifically the transition from muzzle-loading firearms and cannon to breech-loading, rifled small arms and artillery meant weapons became more lethal. As a result, the first major conflict of the industrial age—the American Civil War of 1861–65—resulted in high battle casualties.

Fifty years after the end of the American Civil War, commanders had yet to learn the lessons of that conflict. Then World War I (1914–18) led to bloodshed on an unprecedented scale, when generals continued to throw soldiers at enemy positions—only by this time, weapons were more lethal, such as the machine gun, bolt-action rifle, and quick-firing field artillery.

By the end of World War I, battles were huge and complex, involving hundreds of thousands of soldiers, with airpower adding a new dimension. In World War II (1939–45), technology had advanced to make battles more fluid and decisive, though no less costly in terms of casualties.

The era of the Cold War fortunately avoided a nuclear showdown between the superpowers. However, conflicts still raged around the world as former colonies fought to shake off their European masters.

Over the course of 3,500 years the nature of war has changed but the currency of battle has remained the same: "An army goes into battle; it wins or it loses. Either way, thousands (sometimes tens of thousands) of men die…Every battle casualty is a human being; each is a deep personal tragedy. This is something no reader of military history should ever forget."—Richard Garrett, *Clash of Arms.*

How to use this book

This is a book you can enjoy today, tomorrow, and the whole year round. For each day of the year you will find at least one corresponding entry that tells you about something that happened on that date in history, relating to an epic battle. It might be the end of a war, the death of a great military leader, or the start of a new empire.

You will notice that some dates have a longer entry with a bit more detail to enjoy, while others come with a bonus "also on this day" section when one key event just wasn't enough. Most months have a "one week overview" section, including small snippets of key battle moments from that week throughout history. We recommend enjoying the book by reading one entry each day to build up an interesting picture of battles throughout the year, giving you a fascinating factoid to share on the very day that it happened.

Inspire your colleagues with a regular dose of how the greats got things done; impress your friends with facts galore; and take a moment each day to remember the trailblazers who took charge and changed the world.

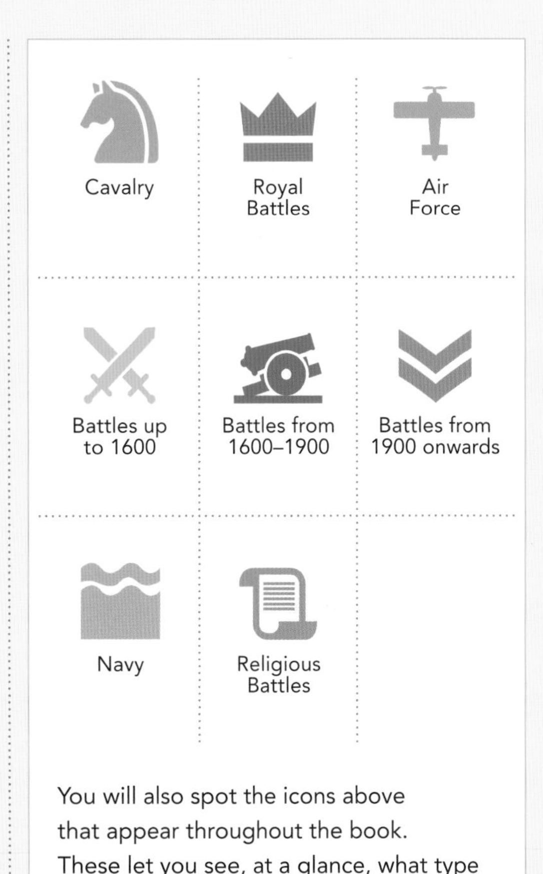

You will also spot the icons above that appear throughout the book. These let you see, at a glance, what type of military event the entry relates to: whether it is a religious, naval, or royal battle. They are also color-coded for your convenience.

CHAPTER 1
January

GERMAN TROOPS DEFEAT THE BRITISH AT CUINCHY

During the first winter of World War I, the weather on the Western Front often proved harder to contend with than the enemy. By the end of 1914, the Allies and the Germans had established themselves in a line of trenches running from the English Channel to the French–Swiss border. Lashing rain and snow, together with the destruction of drainage ditches, led to widespread flooding. At this stage of the war, trenches tended to be simple affairs, but they still required maintaining and repairing.

The village of Cuinchy, 20 miles (32 km) southwest of Lille, was on the front line between the two sides; it was the scene of bitter fighting and was severely damaged. On the first day of the new year, a German attack succeeded in capturing several British positions on a railroad embankment near the shell-blasted ruins of the village, held by the 2nd Brigade of the 1st Division. A British counterattack during the evening failed to retake the positions, as did a second attempt the next day.

▼ A view of a church in ruins, as seen from Old Boots trench in Cuinchy, France.

JANUARY 2

1863

BATTLE OF STONES RIVER General Rosecrans' Union forces defeated the Confederate Army of Tennessee under General Bragg on the outskirts of Murfreesboro, Tennessee.

JANUARY 3

1777

BATTLE OF PRINCETON George Washington defeated the British Army here during the American War of Independence. They retreated from New Jersey to New York.

JANUARY 4

871

FIRST BATTLE OF READING Danish Vikings defeated Alfred the Great, Æthelred, and Æthelwulf's West Saxon force, which tried to storm their camp at Reading, England.

JANUARY 5

1477

SIEGE OF NANCY Charles, Duke of Burgundy, was defeated and killed by the forces of René of Anjou, Duke of Lorraine, and his Swiss allies, while besieging René's capital.

JANUARY 6

1422

BATTLE OF NEBOVIDY The followers of Czech religious reformer Jan Hus used mobile wagon-fortresses to defeat the Imperial forces commanded by Sigismund of Hungary.

JANUARY 7

1745

WAR OF THE AUSTRIAN SUCCESSION An Austrian army surprised the Bavarians in their winter quarters at Amberg, attacking and defeating them.

JANUARY 8

1815

BATTLE OF NEW ORLEANS American troops led by General Jackson defeated British troops under the command of General Pakenham in the last major battle of the War of 1812.

JANUARY 9

1847

U.S. WRESTS CONTROL OF CALIFORNIA FROM THE MEXICANS

The Battle of La Mesa was a small-scale action during the 1422 Mexican–American War. A force of 300 Californio militia, led by General Flores, on horseback and armed only with lances, was defeated by a large force of more than 600 American troops under the command of Commodore Robert F. Stockton. The engagement took place near a ravine where the city of Vernon now stands. The Americans, on foot but equipped with rifles and supported by artillery, quickly got the better of the horsemen, who, despite outflanking and charging the U.S. soldiers, suffered 15 dead and 25 wounded. American casualties were one killed and six wounded. Exhausted and demoralized, the Californios withdrew, many deserting. Flores fled back to Mexico, ceding California to the Americans. On January 13, American control of the state was settled by the signing of the Treaty of Cahuenga.

Exhausted and demoralized, the Californios withdrew, many deserting.

1422

JAN ŽIŽKA DESTROYS THE IMPERIAL ARMY AT NĚMECKÝ BROD

The brilliant Hussite general Jan Žižka came to the fore during the Hussite revolution of 1419 (see January 6, 1422), devising an innovative system of wagon-forts for use on the battlefield against mounted knights, who were until that time the masters of war. The Hussites had scores of horse-drawn wagons filled with crossbowmen and handgunners, which could be moved around the battlefield. When drawn up in a circle and supported by artillery, they were almost invincible.

Following a Hussite victory at Vítkov, which gave them control of Prague, King Sigismund of Hungary (later to become Holy Roman Emperor) invaded Bohemia in 1421. Žižka was at first driven back, but at Německý Brod his wagon-forts inflicted a crushing defeat on the enemy. The outnumbered Hussites destroyed almost half the 23,000-strong Imperial army and Sigismund was forced to retreat from Bohemia.

▼ Historical illustration of the battle at the mountain, Vítkov, Ziskaberg, an earlier battle in the Hussite wars.

1863

UNION VICTORY AT ARKANSAS POST

Arkansas Post, located 50 miles (80 km) up the Arkansas River from Vicksburg, Mississippi, was attacked by 29,000 Union troops commanded by General John McClernand, his troops supported by 13 gunboats. By mid-afternoon, Union artillery had silenced the Confederate guns of Fort Hindman, garrisoned by 4,500 soldiers led by General Thomas Churchill. Under artillery fire and assaulted by thousands of Union soldiers, Hindman surrendered, as did the Confederate troops manning the outlying defenses. The attack cost Union forces 1,600 casualties. Despite the victory, it made the capture of Vicksburg itself no more imminent. So, General Sherman, commander in the West, ordered McClernand to withdraw to concentrate on the far more important objective of Vicksburg.

ALSO ON THIS DAY

1863

At sea, the Confederate commerce raider C.S.S. *Alabama* encounters and sinks the Union steamer U.S.S. *Hatteras* off Galveston Lighthouse, Texas.

1945

JAPAN'S MARITIME SUPPLY NETWORK DAMAGED BY U.S.

The U.S. Navy's Task Force 38, comprising eight fleet carriers, four light carriers, 19 other capital ships, and 56 screening vessels, sailed toward the South China Sea to intercept enemy merchant vessels. The fleet arrived at a point 65 miles (105 km) off Cam Ranh Bay in French Indochina on the morning of January 12, with the aim of attacking Japanese ships moored there.

Reconnaissance indicated that few ships were in the harbor, so instead U.S. carrier aircraft were dispatched to scour for enemy shipping along a 400-mile (640-km) stretch of the Indochinese coast. The U.S. aircraft enjoyed rich pickings. Operating in waves of 30–40 aircraft, they sank 41 Japanese ships, damaged 31 more, and destroyed 112 aircraft on the ground. In addition, docks, oil storage tanks, and airfield facilities were also damaged. The ability of the Japanese to ship essential goods in the South China Sea had been dealt a heavy blow. The engagement was described at the time as "one of the great days of the U.S. Navy."

1849

BRITISH MORALE FALLS AT THE BATTLE OF CHILLIANWALLAH

During the Second Sikh War, in the Punjab region of northwest India, 12,000 British and Bengali troops of the British East India Company, commanded by General Sir Hugh Gough, engaged 35,000 Sikhs, led by General Sher Singh, at almost exactly the same location where the Indians had battled Alexander the Great. A frontal assault by the British ended in disaster. The 24th Foot Regiment's action against Sikh artillery resulted in the loss of 500 officers and men before the regiment was driven back. In addition, following an ineffective cavalry charge, the 14th Light Dragoons were routed. Under pressure from the Sikhs and with darkness approaching, Gough ordered a withdrawal to the starting position, in the wake of 757 killed, 1,651 wounded, and 104 missing. Sikh casualties were at least 4,000 dead and wounded—but British morale had been dealt a heavy blow.

A frontal assault by the British ended in disaster.

1797

NAPOLEON WINS A SPECTACULAR VICTORY AT RIVOLI

During the second year of Napoleon's campaign in northern Italy, the Austrians made a determined effort to relieve the besieged fortress of Mantua. General József Alvinczi led 28,000 troops from Trent down the Adige Valley, planning to break through the bottleneck at Rivoli and head for Mantua. In response, Napoleon hurriedly sent the French divisions of Masséna and Joubert to intercept them at Rivoli, joining them there himself on the evening of the 13th.

Alvinczi's army was in full retreat and Napoleon had won the Battle of Rivoli.

The battle began the next day, the Austrians enjoying some early success. However, determined French resistance, the arrival of reinforcements, and the explosion of two Austrian ammunition wagons which caused chaos among the infantry ranks, resulted in many Austrian units breaking and fleeing. By the late afternoon, Alvinczi's army, now only 13,000-strong, was in full retreat and Napoleon had won the Battle of Rivoli. Mantua surrendered on February 2.

PRUSSIAN TROOPS DEFEAT A FRENCH ATTEMPT TO RELIEVE THE CITY OF BELFORT

The Franco-Prussian War was a disaster and a national humiliation for France, whose desire for revenge would be a contributing factor in the outbreak of World War I more than 40 years later. As Prussian armies advanced into France, the city of Belfort was besieged by 45,000 Prussian troops of XIV Corps. In an effort to break the siege, which had started on November 3, 1870, 110,000 troops of the Army of the East, commanded by General Charles Denis Bourbaki, were launched against the besiegers.

The Battle of the Lisaine River commenced on January 15 in sub-zero conditions. Forest roads were blocked by snowdrifts, which hindered the French assaults. The French made some gains, which were lost when the Prussians counterattacked. The battle would drag on until January 17, by which time the French from Bourbaki down were demoralized, tired, freezing, and hungry. They fled into Switzerland, where they were interned.

▼ The charge of the Prussian infantry at the Battle of the Lisaine River.

1809

THE BRITISH ARMY LOSES ITS COMMANDER AT CORUNNA

Following Napoleon's invasion of Spain in 1808 and his defeat of the Spanish armies facing him, by January 1809 Spain's British allies—35,000 men under Sir John Moore—were in danger of being overrun. Threatened by more than 100,000 French troops led by Napoleon himself, Moore had to retreat to Corunna (A Coruña) in Galicia, northwest Spain, to be evacuated by the Royal Navy.

The British marched into Corunna on January 11, most of them on the verge of exhaustion. The ships had yet to arrive, so Moore deployed his army south of the port, between the village of Elvina and the sea. On the 16th, the pursuing French launched a frontal attack on the British line. The French took the village, were ejected, and took it a second time, before being driven out again by the 42nd Highlanders and 50th Foot led by Moore himself. At the moment of victory, Moore was fatally wounded by a cannonball—but the French had been defeated and the British troops were safely evacuated.

1781

THE BRITISH SUFFER DEFEAT BY AMERICAN TROOPS AT COWPENS

In this engagement during the American War of Independence, Brigadier General Daniel Morgan with 300 Continental riflemen and 700 militiamen faced 1,100 Redcoats and Loyalists, commanded by Lieutenant Colonel Banastre Tarleton. Morgan had intended to attack a British fort, but upon hearing of the approach of Tarleton, moved his army north to Cowpens, South Carolina.

Tarleton escaped; most of his army did not.

When Tarleton arrived, he began skirmishing with the Americans. Morgan's militia, as per orders, fired two shots and fell back. The British, mistaking the withdrawal for a rout, advanced—only to run into a volley of concentrated rifle fire, followed by an American cavalry charge and the return of the militia. The British line was shot to pieces, with more than 800 troops killed, wounded, or captured in a devastating display of the effectiveness of American rifles. American losses were less than 100. Tarleton escaped; most of his army did not.

1955

CHINA AND TAIWAN CLASH AT YIJIANGSHAN

In 1955, the Chinese People's Liberation Army (P.L.A.) launched an amphibious operation to capture fortified Nationalist islands off Taiwan. The two Yijiangshan Islands, 10 miles (16 km) off the Chinese mainland, were garrisoned by 1,000 troops. On January 18 the P.L.A., supported by 184 aircraft, attacked the islands with bombs, backed up by naval gunfire and coastal artillery. The amphibious landing commenced in the afternoon, firepower and numbers overwhelming the garrison. The P.L.A. had 1,500 casualties.

China was preparing to invade more Nationalist islands but, 11 days after the fall of Yijiangshan, the U.S. Congress passed the Formosa Resolution, pledging to defend Taiwan from further attacks. In March, the Americans warned the Communist Chinese they were considering using nuclear weapons to defend the island. In response, Chinese bombardment of Nationalist islands ceased in May 1955.

The islands were attacked with bombs, backed up by naval gunfire and coastal artillery.

1871

THE LAST FRENCH ARMY IS DEFEATED IN THE FRANCO-PRUSSIAN WAR

The Prussian siege of Paris began in September 1870, and all efforts by the French provisional armies to relieve the city had ended in defeat. In January 1871, the last remaining French army in the field, deployed along the Somme River, and numbering around 40,000 men, prepared to march to lift the siege of the French capital, which by now was on the verge of starvation.

Around 40,000 men prepared to march to lift the siege of the French capital.

Commanded by General Louis Faidherbe, it was engaged by a smaller Prussian force under the command of General August von Goeben at Saint-Quentin in northern France. The French were decisively defeated, with 3,500 killed and wounded and a further 9,000 taken prisoner. Prussian casualties were little more than 2,000. The defeat at Saint-Quentin ended all hope of relieving Paris (where riots had now broken out), which surrendered nine days later.

CHILE DEFEATS THE ARMY OF THE PERU–BOLIVIAN CONFEDERATION AT THE BATTLE OF YUNGAY

Chile fought two wars against the combined armies of Peru and Bolivia, considering their efforts to unite their two countries as a grave threat. The first followed the successful efforts of Peru's president, Andrés de Santa Cruz, to engineer a political union between his country and Bolivia.

Chile declared war and invaded Peru, which mobilized 6,000 men in a Confederate army composed of both Peruvians and Bolivians.

Chile declared war and invaded Peru, which mobilized 6,000 men in a Confederate army composed of both Peruvians and Bolivians. The Chilean army numbered 4,500 and was suffering from disease and poor morale. In the initial phase of the Battle of Yungay, the Chileans were worsted and forced to retreat. However, three charges by the Chilean cavalry shattered the Confederate left flank. The entire Confederate battle line then collapsed, suffering 3,000 casualties. The Chileans lost 662 men. Yungay ended the Peru–Bolivian Confederation.

▲ The Battle of Yungay, 1839, ended the confederation of Peru and Bolivia.

1968

THE BATTLE OF KHE SANH BEGINS, HERALDING A 77-DAY SIEGE

The North Vietnamese Army (N.V.A.) launched an assault on the former French outpost at Khe Sanh, located close to the N.V.A.'s primary supply and infiltration route: the Ho Chi Minh Trail in nearby Laos. Defended by U.S. Marines and South Vietnamese Rangers—6,000 men in total—the area around the base was largely jungle, with tall elephant grass and bamboo thickets. This made it easy for the N.V.A. to mass up to 20,000 soldiers around the base.

The base was first hit with hundreds of artillery and mortar rounds and rockets, forcing the defenders to take cover in trenches and bunkers. One of the first rounds hit an ammunition dump near the end of the base's airstrip, causing much devastation. But the disciplined U.S. Marines held their positions, and would continue to do so for the next 77 days. In the Battle of Khe Sanh, 205 U.S. Marines lost their lives. N.V.A. deaths are estimated to be between 10,000 and 15,000 men.

◀ Marines take cover in sandbag shelters as a Communist rocket explodes in the camp at Khe Sanh.

1879

ZULUS WIPE OUT A BRITISH ARMY AT ISANDLWANA

In 1879, Lieutenant General Lord Chelmsford invaded Zululand to coerce the Zulus into joining a federation of British colonies in South Africa. His force was divided into three columns, his own column crossing the Buffalo River and making camp at Isandlwana. On January 22, he led out part of his force to find the Zulu army. But it found him.

Chelmsford had 1,200 men, the infantry armed with breech-loading, single-shot Martini Henry rifles. The majority of the 20,000 Zulus were equipped with short stabbing spears and hide shields. The Zulus advanced on the camp in their traditional formation of central "chest" and right and left "horns." The British infantry opened fire on the chest, forcing the Zulus to go to ground, but the horns raced to find the end of the British line and outflank it. The troops on the British right flank ran out of ammunition and had to return to camp, leaving that flank open. The Zulu chiefs in the center used this opportunity to renew their attack, which forced the British back. Then the horns broke in on each flank. The line collapsed and the Zulus overwhelmed the camp. All but 55 of the British troops were killed. Zulu losses were around 2,000.

JANUARY 23

1942

FOUR U.S. NAVY DESTROYERS LAUNCH A DARING ATTACK OFF THE COAST OF BORNEO

The Battle of Balikpapan was an example of a tactical victory but a strategic defeat. After spotting a Japanese invasion fleet heading for the island of Borneo, a U.S. Navy force of four destroyers and two cruisers, commanded by Rear Admiral William Glassford, was sent to destroy the transports. The cruisers ran into difficulties and had to turn back, leaving the destroyers to attack on their own.

The battle was an example of a tactical victory but a strategic defeat.

The U.S.S. *John D. Ford*, *Pope*, *Parrott*, and *Paul Jones* caught the Japanese fleet at anchor and sank four transports and a patrol boat with their torpedoes for no loss. However, the troops had already been landed and were on their way to conquer Borneo and its oilfields.

▼ Last dash to shore, aboard American-manned Alligators, during the landing of Australian troops at Balikpapan, Borneo.

1597

ANGLO-DUTCH CAVALRY SMASH SPANISH FORCES

During the 80 Years War an Anglo-Dutch force of 6,000 infantry and 800 cavalry under the command of Maurice of Nassau engaged Spanish forces near the city of Turnhout, after making a forced march of 24 miles (38.4 km) in nine hours. The Spanish commander, Count Varax, decided to withdraw his army of 4,000 infantry and 500 cavalry.

The Spanish at first retired in good order, but then the Anglo-Dutch cavalry charged and drove their counterparts off the field, leaving the Spanish infantry isolated. Soon the pistols and carbines were killing many Spaniards, resulting in a rout. The battle had lasted barely half an hour but had cost the Spanish 2,000 dead and wounded, plus 700 captured.

The Spanish at first retired in good order, but then the Anglo-Dutch cavalry charged and drove their counterparts off the field, leaving the Spanish infantry isolated.

1644

THE BATTLE OF NANTWICH ENDS CAVALIER SUPREMACY

The Royalists had captured almost all of the county of Cheshire aside from the town of Nantwich, which had been under siege since December 13. Royalist commander Lord John Byron had 3,500 troops, compared to the Roundhead (Parliamentarian) garrison numbering 1,800. However, Parliamentarian General Sir Thomas Fairfax was marching from Lincolnshire at the head of 5,000 troops to relieve the town.

Alerted to the approach of the relief army, Byron intercepted the Roundheads near Nantwich, in terrain enclosed by hedgerows particularly unsuited to cavalry. In an intense two-hour battle, the Royalist cavalry on the flanks had some success, but in the centre the Roundhead infantry, assisted by the garrison, triumphed. The Royalist foot surrendered, 1,500 of them joining the Parliamentary army.

The battle of Nantwich was the first major Parliamentarian victory in the English Civil War and marked the beginning of the recovery of the Roundhead cause in the north of England. It also enhanced the reputation of Thomas Fairfax, who would become commander of the New Model Army in 1645, leading ultimately to victory for Parliament.

1856

NATIVE AMERICAN RESENTMENT EXPLODES INTO VIOLENCE

The influx of white settlers into Native American lands often led to outbreaks of violence. In January 1856, tensions boiled over when Chiefs Owhi and Leschi led an attack on the town of Seattle. Fortunately for the settlers, they had constructed blockhouses in response to the threat of attack, and the U.S. Navy sloop *Decatur* had been stationed offshore to deter any attacks.

But when on the 26th the Native Americans attacked Seattle, the settlers responded with small-arms fire, and the *Decatur* joined in, firing shells, grapeshot, and canister at the attackers. Two settlers were killed before the Native Americans were driven off after losing around 200 warriors. Owhi was later captured and killed, and Leschi was hanged.

ALSO ON THIS DAY

1564

Lithuanian troops surprise and defeat a large invading Russian force at the Battle of Ula, during the Livonian War. The Russians are unarmed.

1868

SAMURAI CLASH AT TOBA-FUSHIMI DURING THE BOSHIN WAR

In January 1868, the final Shogun, Tokugawa Yoshinobu, ceded authority to the young emperor, Meiji, aged 15. This resulted in a clash, and eventually war, between modernizers and traditionalists in the emperor's council.

The Shogun's 15,000 samurai, equipped with swords, spears, and bows faced the pro-Imperial army of 5,000 men, with British howitzers and French rifles.

The four-day battle of Toba-Fushimi pitted the pro-Imperial army of 5,000 men, possessing British howitzers and French rifles, against the Shogun's 15,000 samurai equipped with swords, spears, and bows. On the 27th, the Shogun's troops tried to force a crossing of the Koeda Bridge in South Kyoto, and were slaughtered. The Shogun went on to lose the battle, signaling Japan's entry into the modern era.

A RAGTAG GROUP OF BOER FARMERS RESIST THE MIGHT OF THE BRITISH EMPIRE AT LAING'S NEK

In the northern tip of Natal, South Africa, 1,200 British troops advancing to relieve garrisons in the Transvaal ran into a force of around 2,000 Boers at the pass of Laing's Nek in the Drakensberg Mountains. The Boers, led by Commandant General P. J. Joubert, who were nothing more than a citizen militia armed with hunting rifles, had occupied the hills overlooking the road the British were marching along.

The British commander, Major General Colley, like many of his contemporaries, was contemptuous of the Boers, and immediately sent forward mounted troops to attack them, without success. The British infantry wore red jackets and blue trousers, making them easier to aim at. Next to attack was the 58th Regiment, which the Boers proceeded to shoot to pieces as it advanced uphill carrying its colors (this was the last time a British regiment took its colors into action). The regiment abandoned the attack and retreated back down the hill. The battle was over, the British suffering 198 casualties, the Boers 41.

The Battle of Laing's Nek was the first time that British soldiers suffered at the hands of skilled Boer marksmen. A month later, Colley was killed at the Battle of Majuba Hill, which ended the First Boer War.

▼ Illustration of the Assembly of Boers before the evacuation of Laing's Nek, March 24, 1881, in Transvaal, South Africa.

1814

NAPOLEON'S FLEDGLINGS ROUT PRUSSIA'S VETERANS

Brienne was Napoleon's first major battle of the 1814 campaign in France, a campaign fought against an enemy coalition with overwhelming numbers and with a French army greatly lacking in cavalry and experienced soldiers. Deciding that the best form of defense was attack, Napoleon struck east at the head of 36,000 troops, many of them youngsters just out of recruiting camps and with no military experience. At Brienne, he ran into a 28,000-strong Russo-Prussian army, commanded by the Prussian Marshal Blücher.

The battle raged throughout the day, the French recruits acquitting themselves honorably against veteran Russian and Prussian troops. Eventually, Blücher, who had narrowly avoided capture, disengaged and retreated southeast toward the main Austrian army (curiously, Napoleon himself was almost captured by Cossacks the day after the battle). The result was a narrow French victory, Napoleon losing 3,000 men and the Allies around 4,000. The French emperor had failed in his attempt to trap and destroy Blücher's army, but the battle had greatly boosted the morale of his inexperienced recruits, who would go on to perform heroic battlefield exploits during the rest of the campaign.

1968

THE TET OFFENSIVE BEGINS

The Tet Offensive was a series of coordinated attacks carried out by the North Vietnamese Army (N.V.A.) and Viet Cong guerrillas throughout South Vietnam. The U.S. and South Vietnamese militaries sustained heavy losses before defeating the Communist offensive. The Viet Cong was all but wiped out during Tet, but it played a pivotal role in weakening U.S. public support for America's involvement in the Vietnam War.

The U.S. and South Vietnamese militaries sustained heavy losses.

Viet Cong attacks in Hue and Saigon (where they assaulted the U.S. Embassy) shocked both the U.S. military and the public back home. Though Tet had been a tactical disaster for the N.V.A. and Viet Cong, it greatly influenced President Johnson's decision to press for peace in Vietnam, his pledge to stop bombing North Vietnam, and his declaration that he would not seek another term as president. For the Americans, after Tet the problem became not how to win the war but how to disengage.

BRITISH COMMONWEALTH FORCES WIN A MAJOR VICTORY AGAINST THE ITALIANS AT AGORDAT

Mussolini's colony in the Horn of Africa, Italian East Africa, was the scene of a decisive victory for Commonwealth and British forces when they defeated the Italians at the city of Agordat.

The Commonwealth forces had launched an assault against Italian East Africa in January 1941, the Italian commander, General Orlando Lorenzini, withdrawing his troops back into Ethiopia and Eritrea, and eventually concentrating his defense around the city of Agordat in Eritrea.

The defenders, who were exhausted following a 125-mile (200-km) retreat, numbered around 7,000, with 76 artillery pieces and a few companies of light and medium tanks. Facing them were General Beresford-Peirse's 4th Indian Division, supported by aircraft of the South African Air Force.

Launching their attack on the 31st, the 4th Indian Division soon broke through the Italian defenses, its Matilda tanks demoralizing the Italians, whose artillery and tank shells bounced off their armor. The Italian M11/39 medium tanks proved no match for the Matildas, 11 being knocked out in quick succession for no British losses. Lorenzini ordered a retreat, but 2,000 of his men were captured at Agordat, together with most of his tanks and artillery pieces.

▲ Italian M11/39 tanks captured after the Battle of Agordat.

CHAPTER 2

February

FEBRUARY 1 1940

THE RED ARMY UNLEASHES HELL AGAINST THE FINNS

The Second Battle of Summa would decide the outcome of the Winter War between Finland and the U.S.S.R. Following a series of defeats against the small, poorly armed Finnish Army in 1939, the Red Army had undergone intensive training in January 1940, preparing for offensives by coordinating tanks, infantry, and artillery to overwhelm Finnish positions. Mass attacks were abandoned in favor of using artillery to destroy enemy positions before the infantry and tanks went in.

On February 1, the Soviet 13th and 7th Armies launched their attack in Karelia, with a total of 600,000 troops. The Finns had six divisions in line and a further three in reserve. In 1939, massed Red Army infantry attacks had been shot to pieces by Finnish artillery and small-arms fire. But now the tables were turned: The Red Army first pounded the Finnish positions with 300,000 artillery shells, after which the defenders were strafed by close-support aircraft. The 13th Army attacked between Taipale and Lake Muolaanjärvi, the 7th assaulting in the Summa sector. Finnish positions were pounded and overwhelmed over several days, signaling the Red Army's eventual victory in the Finnish campaign—though it would take a further month of fighting before the Finns requested an armistice.

▼ Soviet T-26 light tanks and GAZ-A trucks of the Soviet 7th Army during its advance on the Karelian Isthmus.

THE END COMES AT STALINGRAD

The titanic battle of Stalingrad came to an end when the last remnants of the German 6th Army surrendered to the Russians. In total, 150,000 Germans were killed and another 90,000 taken prisoner during the battle for the city of Stalingrad. The Luftwaffe lost 488 aircraft and 1,000 aircrew while trying to keep the trapped 6th Army supplied.

> **"We will fight to the last man, but we shall not leave the city."**
>
> —RODIMTZEV

Stalingrad was one of the decisive battles of World War II, which shattered notions of German invincibility and weakened the Wehrmacht to such an extent that it would never again be able to launch an offensive all along the Eastern Front. The initiative now passed to the rejuvenated Red Army, only to be squandered in the early months of 1943 due to Stalin's overconfidence.

▼ Red Army troops move through the rubble of Stalingrad following the German surrender in 1943. The Soviets had an estimated 1.1 million casualties during the six-month campaign.

1706

FIFTEEN MINUTES OF SLAUGHTER

At Fraustadt (present-day Wschowa) in Poland, during the Great Northern War, Swedish forces annihilated an army of Saxon and Russian troops. Though all armies in the conflict were armed and equipped in a similar fashion, Swedish tactics placed the emphasis on attack at all times. Thus when 10,000 Swedes commanded by Field Marshal Rehnsköld encountered a Russo-Saxon army of 18,000 under Johann Matthias von Schulenburg at Fraustadt, it immediately attacked. The Swedish cavalry on the wings drove off their opponents and then assisted their own infantry in the center. The Russians and Saxons, surrounded, were massacred in 15 minutes of combat, up to 8,000 being killed and 6,000 captured. Fraustadt marked Sweden's high point in the war.

Russian soldiers were dressed in white coats with red lining, with some during the retreat having turned their coats inside out to resemble Saxons in the hope of mercy.

634

HOLY WAR BEGINS AT DATHIN

In the early seventh century, following the unification of the Arabian Peninsula under the Islamic religion, Abu Bakr, father-in-law of the prophet Muhammad and first caliph after the latter's death, summoned the faithful to wage holy war—*jihad*—against the infidel. This resulted in a battle at the village of Dathin, near Gaza, between Arab forces and soldiers of the Byzantine Empire. The Byzantine force of 5,000 troops was led by the regional commander, Sergius; the Arabs, who could muster only 1,000 men, led by Yazid ibn Abi Sufyan. On receiving reports of the advance of the Arab force, Sergius left his base at Caesarea with 300 cavalry and rode to Gaza, where he gathered his army.

The details of the resulting battle at Dathin are sketchy, but it appears that the Arabs sprang an ambush on the Byzantine army while it was on the march. The first to be struck by the attackers were the Byzantine foot soldiers, who were cut down. Seeing this, Sergius apparently fled for his life, but was caught by the pursuing Arabs and killed.

Dathin was a relatively minor affair, but was celebrated in the Arab world as the first Muslim victory in the holy war against the infidels.

BATTLE AMONG THE PADDY FIELDS

This day signaled the start of the Battle of the Admin Box, fought in northern Arakan in Burma. A motley collection of British clerks, drivers, and doctors, stiffened by a smattering of infantry and tank crews, fought off a series of attacks by Japanese infantry in one of the most amazing battles of World War II.

The battle's name refers to the administration area of the Indian Army's 7th Division. For the most part it was fought hand-to-hand in the paddy fields. When it ended on February 23, 5,000 Japanese soldiers lay dead on the battlefield. For the first time in the Burma campaign, the vaunted Japanese Army had been defeated.

ALSO ON THIS DAY

1941

The Battle of Keren, part of the East Africa Campaign in World War II, begins. Fighting ends on April 1, 1941, the British having defeated the Italians.

FIRST BLOOD FOR THE UNION

Fort Henry was a Confederate fort on the Tennessee River. On February 4–5, Union general Ulysses S. Grant landed his troops on the east bank of the Tennessee River and on high ground on the Kentucky side of the river. Supported by seven gunboats, which began bombarding the fort, Grant launched his attack. The fort's commander, Brigadier General Lloyd Tilghman, quickly surrendered.

It was the first important Federal victory of the war and the first victory for General Grant.

The Battle of Fort Henry was important because it opened the Tennessee and Columbia Rivers to Union gunboats and shipping for the rest of the Civil War. It was the first important Federal victory of the war and the first victory for General Grant.

1915

A STORM OF SNOW AND LEAD

The Second, or Winter, Battle of the Masurian Lakes began in a blinding snowstorm. Determined to knock Russia out of World War I, Germany's Field Marshal Paul von Hindenburg launched his 8th and 10th Armies against the Russian 10th Army north of the Masurian Lakes on the Eastern Front.

On the first day, German troops of the 8th Army overwhelmed Russian lines. The German 10th Army went in on the following day, also scattering Russian forces. But heroic defense by the 20th Corps averted a total Russian collapse, holding out until February 21 before they finally surrendered. Nevertheless, the Russian Army had suffered 200,000 casualties in a major defeat. German losses in battle were light, but many troops suffered from exposure due to the freezing weather.

“Fighting the Russians, we had to remove the piles of enemy bodies from before our trenches, so as to get a clear field of fire against new waves of assault.”

—PAUL VON HINDENBURG

1807

NAPOLEON'S FIRST SETBACK IN BATTLE

French emperor Napoleon clashed with the Russian general Bennigsen at the Battle of Eylau (now Bagrationovsk). Some 45,000 French troops faced 67,000 Russians across a frozen battlefield.

The 3rd Corps had more success against the Russian left flank, but the arrival of 7,000 Prussian troops prevented a French victory.

Following heavy artillery bombardment, the French 7th Corps struck the Russian center during a blinding snowstorm but was beaten off with heavy losses. The 3rd Corps had more success against the Russian left flank, but the arrival of 7,000 Prussian troops prevented a French victory. Darkness and exhaustion brought the battle to a close.

This indecisive battle was Napoleon's first check on the battlefield and cost him 20,000 casualties. Russian losses were lower, at 15,000.

1904

RUSSIAN NAVAL HEROISM

During the Russo-Japanese War of 1904–5, Russian's second-rate navy was worsted by Japan's modern warships. Nothing illustrates the gulf in class between the two than the Battle of Chemulpo Bay.

***Korietz*, sheltering near an island, suffered no damage but followed the *Varyag* back to port, where both ships were scuttled.**

The landing of Japanese troops in Korea near Chemulpo (present-day Incheon) prompted two Russian warships in the port, the cruiser *Varyag* and the gunboat *Korietz*, to sail out to battle the 15 Japanese warships positioned offshore. The *Varyag* was badly damaged in the brief battle, all her main guns being put out of action and 33 of her 500-man crew being killed. *Korietz*, sheltering near an island, suffered no damage but followed the *Varyag* back to port, where both ships were scuttled.

1846

SIKH TWILIGHT

In what was to be the final battle of the First Anglo-Sikh War, a 15,000-strong Anglo-Indian army under the command of General Hugh Gough defeated 25,000 Sikhs near the Sutlej River, at Sobraon in the East Punjab. The Sikh position comprised a semicircular ditch and earth rampart around a bend in the river. Making a feint toward the Sikhs' right flank, Gough struck their left flank hard, driving the defenders from their entrenchments. The Sikh battle line began to collapse, thousands fleeing and plunging into the river. An estimated 9,000 Sikhs were killed in combat or drowned in the Sutlej while trying to escape. British and Indian losses amounted to 2,283.

ALSO ON THIS DAY

1814

At the Battle of Champaubert, Napoleon inflicts a sharp defeat on a Russian army under the command of General Olsufiev. Believing the Prussians will come to his aid, he elects to hold his position, whereupon he is beaten and his entire force captured by the French.

1814

NAPOLEON: MASTER OF WAR

Montmirail, a village between the Marne and Seine rivers, was the location of a battle where Napoleon maneuvered brilliantly to temporarily check the Allied invasion of France.

By skillful positioning, Napoleon got his forces into the middle of the widely scattered Prussian Army of Silesia. Though outnumbered, the French emperor led 20,000 troops against Prussian and Russian forces in the Montmirail area. At first, the Russian forces prevailed against the French, and the approach of Prussian troops seemed to herald an Allied victory. But the Prussians were marching on a muddy track and their progress was slow, allowing the French to break through the Russian line. The Russian commander, Prince Fabian von Osten-Sacken, launched a desperate counterattack, which was thrown back with the assistance of the French Imperial Guard.

The eventual arrival of the Prussians allowed the shattered Russians to escape the field after suffering 4,000 casualties. French losses were half that, while the Prussians suffered 900 killed.

Napoleon was again triumphant against the Russians and Prussians on February 12, at the Battle of Château-Thierry; though, once again, he failed to annihilate the enemy army, which meant the War of the Sixth Coalition would continue in the Allies' favor.

▼ A somber-looking Napoleon at the head of his staff during the 1814 campaign, in which the French emperor outmaneuvered his enemies many times.

1817

CHILE'S FIGHT FOR FREEDOM

Following Napoleon's invasion of Spain in 1808, many of Spain's colonies in South America seized the opportunity to assert their claims of independence. Chile was one such colony, though it would take ten years of fighting before the country would escape the Spanish yoke. A major stepping stone to that goal took place at the Battle on Chacabuco in 1817.

Following his victory over the Spanish in Argentina, José de San Martín assembled an army of 6,000 men to liberate Chile from the Spanish. He crossed the mountain range at the beginning of 1817, with his Army of the Andes losing a third of his men to the extreme weather conditions. Once over the mountains, he linked up with a Chilean army under the leadership of Bernardo O'Higgins, a wealthy Chilean patriot of Irish descent. Their combined army of 3,600 troops engaged a Spanish army numbering 2,500 troops under General Maroto in the valley of Chacabuco near Santiago. O'Higgins, showing his inexperience, led his 1,500 men forward in a wild charge, forcing San Martín to support him. The battle raged on into the afternoon, the Spanish eventually being overwhelmed as they held a defensive square around the Chacabuco Ranch. A total of 500 were killed and 600 captured. The Army of the Andes suffered only 132 fatalities.

1951

THE GETTYSBURG OF THE KOREAN WAR

Thousands of Chinese troops attacked the U.S. Army's understrength 23rd Infantry Regiment around the village of Chipyong-ni. The Chinese launched their first attack during the evening, thousands of troops advancing against the 4,500 U.S. soldiers. The Americans used "fougasse drums"—improvised explosive devices which they detonated using grenades to spray the Chinese with burning petrol and oil. The battle lasted into the morning of the next day, the Chinese finally retreating. They attacked again during the evening of the 14th, withdrawing again on the 15th when U.S. aircraft dropped napalm on them. The result of the Battle of Chipyong-ni was 51 dead and 250 wounded Americans, and 1,000 dead and 2,000 wounded Chinese.

The Chinese launched their first attack during the evening, thousands of troops advancing against the 4,500 U.S. soldiers.

1797

THE NELSON TOUCH

The Battle of Cape St. Vincent pitted the British Royal Navy against a Spanish fleet off the southwest coast of Portugal.

Nelson captured two Spanish vessels, the *San Nicolás* and *San José*, and other Royal Navy ships captured two additional enemy ships.

The British fleet of 21 ships commanded by Admiral Sir John Jervis engaged the Spanish fleet of Admiral Don José de Córdoba (35 ships) 25 miles (37.5 km) offshore. The Spanish were heading for the port of Cádiz in two sections when, without waiting for orders, a certain Commodore Horatio Nelson led an attack in his ship *Captain* on the larger section. To achieve greatest impact, Royal Navy ships held their fire until alongside the Spanish ships before firing their broadsides. In the ensuing battle, Nelson captured two Spanish vessels, the *San Nicolás* and *San José*, and other Royal Navy ships captured a further two enemy ships with no loss.

1944

PUMMELING MONTE CASSINO

During the Italian campaign in World War II, Allied forces were held up at the German Gustav Line for five months in 1944. One key point in the German defense was the monastery atop Monte Cassino, which initially was not defended by German troops.

The Allies started the Second Battle of Monte Cassino by unleashing 230 bombers while the artillery of II Corps pounded the monastery and surrounding area. When the bombing had finished, the 4th Indian Division attacked, to be repulsed with heavy loss by German paratroopers who had been sheltering in the monastery's subterranean chambers. Allied attacks ended on February 18, the monastery still in German hands.

ALSO ON THIS DAY

1898

The explosion that ignited a war.
The battleship U.S.S. *Maine* explodes and sinks in Havana harbor, Cuba, leading to the United States declaring war on Spain.

1646

THE FORGOTTEN BATTLE OF THE ENGLISH CIVIL WAR

In the dying embers of the Civil War, the town of Torrington, Devon, was in the hands of what remained of the Royalist Army in the west. The Parliamentarian general Thomas Fairfax, determined to crush this last pocket of Cavaliers, marched from Exeter with 10,000 troops. In the early hours of February 16, the Roundheads attacked the town, regiments of foot and horse breaking through the Royalist barricades. Fierce fighting followed in Torrington's streets. A church in which Royalist prisoners were being held blew up when gunpowder stored inside it was ignited. The explosion ended the battle, the remaining Cavaliers fleeing for their lives.

ALSO ON THIS DAY

1270

At the Battle of Karuse, soldiers of the Grand Duchy of Lithuania defeat the Crusader knights of the Livonian Order on the frozen Baltic Sea between the island of Muhu and the mainland.

1461

BLOOD IN THE STREETS

Following her victory at Wakefield during the Wars of the Roses, Queen Margaret's Lancastrian army of 14,000 marched south toward London to free King Henry VI from the Yorkists. Barring their way was a Yorkist army of 10,000 men under the Earl of Warwick, which marched from London to St. Albans, 20 miles (32 km) from the capital. The Lancastrians, who had outflanked Warwick's defenses, stormed into the town. Initially they suffered heavy casualties from Yorkist archers who had been billeted there, and for several hours the battle hung in the balance. Fierce hand-to-hand fighting resulted in the archers being cut down, however, and the Lancastrians prevailed.

Warwick, having lost 4,000 men, broke off the battle and retreated to London, barely escaping with his life. The Yorkists left behind King Henry, Margaret's husband, who according to legend watched the battle while sitting under a tree, singing to himself.

The united king and queen could have entered London unopposed and brought the war to an end, but instead marched back north. This allowed Warwick to regroup in London where he was joined by Edward, Duke of York (who should have joined him at St. Albans), who proclaimed himself King Edward IV.

FIRST BRITISH VICTORY OVER THE BOERS

The Battle of Paardeberg clearly illustrates that British commanders of the late 19th century had yet to learn the futility of throwing infantry against an enemy armed with modern weapons in entrenched positions.

Following the relief of Kimberley in the Orange Free State, the Boer commander in the region, General Piet Cronjé, withdrew his 5,000 Boers to Paardeberg on the banks of the Modder River. His march had been slow, however, which allowed the troops of General Lord Roberts, who had invaded the Orange Free State, to surround Cronjé's forces. The battle began in the early hours of February 18, British artillery blowing Boer wagons and their oxen to pieces. Had the British relied solely on their artillery, they might have forced the surrender of the Boers that day. But the Boers were reprieved by the arrival of Lord Kitchener, whom Roberts put in temporary command. Kitchener launched four infantry brigades against the Boers, losing 1,000 men in futile frontal attacks. Roberts eventually called off these attacks and returned to shelling the Boer positions with his artillery. After ten days of bombardment, Cronjé surrendered on February 27.

▲ The Battle of Paardeberg, South Africa. Artwork by Richard Knotel.

1945

STORMING THE BEACHES AT IWO JIMA

The U.S. V Amphibious Corps was the force which fought the Battle of Iwo Jima in 1945, one of the bloodiest clashes of the Pacific War.

A total of 70,000 U.S. Marines were tasked with seizing the island, which was only 760 miles (1,222 km) from Tokyo itself. Defending Iwo Jima were 20,000 troops under the command of Lieutenant General Tadamichi Kuribayashi. The Japanese had embarked upon an intensive program of strengthening the island's defenses with pillboxes and strongpoints, which would slow the American advance and inflict heavy casualties on the Marines.

The Battle of Iwo Jima in 1945 was one of the bloodiest clashes of the Pacific War.

Though the island had been bombarded beforehand by B-29 heavy bombers and by naval artillery, when the Marines landed on Iwo Jima they came under intense enemy fire that killed 2,500. Nevertheless, by the end of the day 30,000 Marines had been landed on the beaches. They would go on to take the island despite fierce resistance.

1653

THE ENGLISH REGAIN CONTROL OF THE CHANNEL

The Battle of Portland, which concluded on February 20 after a three-day fight, was the fourth engagement in the First Anglo-Dutch War. It resulted in the English regaining control of the English Channel, which had been lost after the Dutch victory at Dungeness in 1652.

An English fleet under the command of Admiral Robert Blake was attacked by Dutch ships led by Admiral Maarten Tromp, which were escorting 200 merchantmen through the English Channel. The English fleet numbered 80 ships and was divided into three squadrons: Red, White, and Blue. The English warships mounted between 40 and 60 cannon. Tromp had 75 warships but hoped to avoid a battle by sailing through the English Channel before the English put to sea. But bad weather and stragglers wrecked his plan. In the three-day running battle, the Dutch lost four warships captured, five sunk, and two more burned. In addition, some 40 merchant ships were captured. Blake lost two ships and three others needed major repairs; Blake himself was badly wounded.

Victory at Portland and later at the Gabbard in June 1653 allowed the English to win the war by imposing a blockade on Holland.

FRUITLESS CARNAGE AT VERDUN

The Battle of Verdun in 1916 is the epitome of the futile waste of lives during World War I. Determined to break the deadlock on the Western Front, the German Chief of Staff, General Erich von Falkenhayn, organized a massive assault on the Verdun salient held by the French 2nd Army. The German 5th Army of one million men, commanded by Crown Prince Friedrich Wilhelm, was the instrument by which Falkenhayn would bleed the French army white.

On February 21, the first day of the battle, 1,400 German artillery pieces pounded the French lines for 12 hours on an 8-mile (12.8 km) front east of the Meuse River. Then the infantry attacked, only to run into the predictable machine-gun and artillery fire. Verdun thus became yet another grim slugging match where thousands of lives were lost for a few yards of ground gained each day. The crown prince, from his position several miles behind the front, persisted in throwing his men at French positions, oblivious to the cost.

By the time German attacks at Verdun ceased on July 11, 1916, the Kaiser's men had advanced around 4 miles (6.5 km) in total, at a price of 280,000 casualties. The French, who had been under the resolute command of General Philippe Pétain, suffered 315,000 casualties.

▲ French troops under shellfire during the Battle of Verdun.

1847

SANTA ANNA'S FOLLY, AMERICA'S GAIN

The Mexican–American War of 1846–48 was a disaster for Mexico, partly because of America's fervor to fulfill its "manifest destiny" to expand its territory across the entire North American continent, but also because of inept Mexican military leadership. A case in point is the Battle of Buena Vista, a two-day event that began on February 22, 1847.

General Zachary Taylor, in northern Mexico with 4,800 inexperienced U.S. troops, disobeyed orders to remain on the defensive and instead marched southeast. Sensing an easy victory, the Mexican General Santa Anna collected 20,000 soldiers at San Luis Potosí and began marching north to intercept Taylor. In response, Taylor withdrew to a defile a short distance from the village of Buena Vista, in the state of Coahuila.

Santa Anna marched rapidly to arrive at Buena Vista with more than 14,000 men, demanding that the Americans surrender. Taylor refused, whereupon Santa Anna attacked. However, so exhausted were his soldiers that they could not take advantage of their superiority in numbers. When the two-day battle ended, the Mexicans had been defeated, losing 500 killed and 1,000 wounded. U.S. losses were 267 killed and 456 wounded. This battle ended the war in northern Mexico.

1885

THE BATTLE TO DECIDE THE FATE OF VIETNAM

The Sino-French War in the 1880s was fought to decide who should control Vietnam. The French army and navy were equipped with modern weapons which made them more than a match for the poorly-armed Chinese army.

On February 23, 1885, French troops of the Tonkin Expeditionary Corps defeated an army of Chinese troops at the town of Dong Dang in northern Tonkin, close to the border between Vietnam and China. The 6,000 Chinese troops, part of the Guangxi Army, took up a strong position centered on a limestone plateau that could only be accessed on its western side. Their right wing was deployed in and around Dong Dang. The French commander, General de Négrier, had 2,900 men, supported by artillery.

The battle opened with the Chinese launching two flanking attacks, which the French defeated. But to win the battle, de Négrier realized he had to eject the Chinese from the plateau, which required taking Dong Dang itself. In front of the town was a stream, which French troops reached and forded under enemy fire from the plateau. The infantry then rushed into Dong Dang, killing the defenders, before ascending the plateau under enemy fire. Such was the speed of the French advance that they suffered only light casualties: nine dead and 46 wounded in total.

1525

THE DAY OF THE ARQUEBUSIERS

▲ Francis I of France became a prisoner at the Battle of Pavia, on February 24, 1525.

The Battle of Pavia was the decisive clash of the French war in Italy, resulting in French defeat and the capture of its king.

The battle was a milestone in the development of warfare, illustrating that firepower could triumph over cavalry if used correctly. When King Francis I of France laid siege to the Italian city of Pavia, an Imperial army of 23,000, mostly Spaniards, was assembled to relieve it. Francis, commanding 23,500 men, deployed his army to face the Spaniards concentrated to the north of Pavia. His artillery caused disorder among the Spanish, allowing his mounted knights to charge and scatter a Spanish division. Francis then brought up his fearsome Swiss pikemen, who charged at the Spanish infantry in a frontal assault, only to be shot to pieces by the firepower of the arquebusiers (armed with a smoothbore firearm called an arquebus). As the battle raged, the 1,500 Spanish arquebusiers raked the French line from the flank, which collapsed. The Spanish charged and won the battle, capturing Francis and proving the superiority of firepower over traditional styles of warfare.

1704

THE APALACHEE MASSACRE

A raiding party of 50 British colonists and 1,000 of their Creek allies attacked the Spanish mission town of Ayubale in Apalachee Province, Florida, to punish the Spanish for inciting Native American attacks against English settlers. The raiding party was led by James Moore, who was determined to finance his expedition by seizing Spanish gold and native slaves. The Battle of Ayubale was in reality a massacre, Moore killing the defenders, headed by Father Ángel Miranda, after they had surrendered. When a relief force of 30 Spanish cavalry and 400 Apalachee warriors arrived, 200 of the latter were killed by Moore's forces.

1991

TANK BATTLE AT 73 EASTING

Two days after the Allied forces launched their ground offensive during the Persian Gulf War, also called the Gulf War, the last great tank battle of the 20th century was fought. The 2nd Armored Cavalry Regiment, equipped with Abrams tanks, spearheaded the advance of the U.S. 7th Corps. On arrival at a spot designated as 73 Easting, it ran into Iraqi tanks. What followed was a huge tank battle in which the Abrams knocked out 160 Iraqi tanks, 180 armored personnel carriers, and 12 artillery pieces for no loss. Two brigades of the Iraqi Republican Guard were wiped out in a demoralizing defeat for Saddam Hussein's elite formation.

▼ An Iraqi Type 69 main battle tank burns after an attack at 73 Easting, during Operation Desert Storm.

1942

JAPANESE HIGH TIDE IN THE PACIFIC

In February 1942, the Allies established naval units for the protection of Java. The Eastern Striking Force—five cruisers and nine destroyers—under Dutch Rear Admiral Karel Doorman sailed to intercept a Japanese force of four cruisers and 14 destroyers escorting 41 transport vessels headed for Java.

At around 14:00 hours on the 27th, the two forces met in what became known as the Battle of the Java Sea. The battle lasted seven hours and at any time Doorman could have broken off contact and withdrawn. However, he was determined to achieve a decisive result and got one: a Japanese victory. After the battle, the Japanese convoy sailed on and began landing troops the next day. The outgunned Allied ships suffered badly during the action, two Dutch cruisers being sunk (Doorman went down with one of them), the British cruiser *Exeter* badly damaged, and three destroyers sunk. Some 2,300 Allied sailors died in the battle, compared to only 36 Japanese.

The outgunned Allied ships suffered badly during the action.

1991

THE MOTHER OF ALL BATTLES

The combat phase of the Gulf War, codenamed Operation Desert Storm, ended on this day. In response to Iraqi dictator Saddam Hussein's invasion of Kuwait in August 1990, a United Nations (U.N.) coalition was formed to eject the Iraqis from the country. Eventually, U.N. forces assembled in Saudi Arabia totaled 750,000, including 540,000 U.S. personnel.

When the ground offensive was launched in February, Iraqi opposition was easily swept aside.

Prior to Desert Storm, the Iraqis were first hit by air strikes, which destroyed their command and communications network, degraded their armored assets, and demoralized their soldiers. When the ground offensive was launched in February, Iraqi opposition was easily swept aside. In the space of a few days, U.N. forces had decimated the Iraqi Army with Iraqi deaths estimated at over 50,000. Just 292 U.N. men were killed.

CHAPTER 3

March

ITALIAN DEBACLE AT ADOWA

King of Kings Menelik II overthrew Italian control over Ethiopia in 1895. In response, the Italian government sent an army to Africa under the command of General Oreste Baratieri. On March 1, 1896, underestimating the Ethiopians, Baratieri deployed his men into several columns to converge on the high ground overlooking the town of Adowa, where the Ethiopians had assembled. What followed was a disaster for the Italians. Their columns became lost and confused, inviting the Ethiopians to attack. In total, 100,000 warriors, many armed with rifles, wiped out the Italian army, 6,000 of the 17,000 engaged being killed, 1,500 wounded, and 3,000 taken prisoner in a humiliating defeat.

▼ Italian and Ethiopian soldiers fighting during the Battle of Adowa.

1476

SWISS REVENGE OVER CHARLES OF BURGUNDY

Medieval warfare was often brutal, particularly regarding the treatment of prisoners. When Charles the Bold, Duke of Burgundy, captured the Swiss castle of Grandson in 1476, he had the entire garrison executed after it had surrendered. Unfortunately for Charles, a Swiss relief army then appeared, which resulted in the Battle of Grandson fought on March 2.

When Charles the Bold captured the Swiss castle of Grandson in 1476, he had the entire garrison executed after it had surrendered.

When the Swiss pikemen and halbardiers arrived, Charles formed up his veteran army to give battle, but the Swiss phalanx beat off two Burgundian cavalry charges. Charles then planned to pull back his center to lure the Swiss forward, after which his flanks would swing inward to destroy them. But the appearance of two further Swiss units caused panic among the Burgundians, leading to a rout.

1944

MERRILL'S MARAUDERS ON THE RAMPAGE

On this day, Chinese Army chief of staff Joseph W. Stilwell began the Battle of Maingkwan–Walawbum in the Hukawng Valley of northern Burma. Using his Chinese 22nd and 38th Divisions to mount a frontal assault, he sent the U.S. Army's 5307th Composite Unit, nicknamed "Merrill's Marauders," on a flanking attack to trap the Japanese 18th Division. The tactic nearly worked, but a combination of inhospitable terrain and tenacious Japanese resistance enabled Major General Shinichi Tanaka to extract his division, albeit with some difficulty.

Merrill's Marauders was a special operations jungle warfare unit created by General Frank Merrill in 1943.

The tactic nearly worked, but a combination of inhospitable terrain and tenacious Japanese resistance enabled Major General Shinichi Tanaka to extract his division.

1238

INVASION OF THE MONGOL HORDES

The fast-moving and expertly trained Mongol horse warriors swept the medieval world like a hurricane, obliterating all who stood in their way. One such region was the Russian principality of Vladimir–Suzdal, which was invaded by a Mongol army led by Batu Khan, a grandson of Genghis Khan, in 1238.

Grand Prince Yuri II fled north across the Volga River when the Mongols sacked his capital, Vladimir. He hastily mustered an army, but, like many medieval armies, it was a mixture of good troops and poor levies, and was no match for the battle-hardened Mongols. On March 4, 10,000 Mongol horsemen surrounded Yuri's force of 3,000 at the Sit River. Yuri lost his head and his army was annihilated.

ALSO ON THIS DAY

1814

The Battle of Longwoods, during the Anglo-American War of 1812, results in a British defeat at the hands of a force of American cavalry. The battle took place near Wardsville, modern-day Middlesex County, Ontario, Canada.

1811

CLIPPING BONAPARTE'S WINGS

By the end of 1810, Napoleon had conquered most of Spain and his brother sat on the Spanish throne. Only the besieged port of Cádiz, temporary home to the Spanish government, held out.

The Battle of Barrosa began when a force of 15,000 Spanish, Portuguese, and British troops under General Thomas Graham was landed along the coast with the intention of raising the siege. However, the French commander, Marshal Victor, ambushed the force with 10,000 men at Barrosa Ridge, routing the Spanish. Graham then led his 500 British troops in a counterattack that drove the French from the ridge, winning the Battle of Barrosa where, for the first time in the Peninsular War, a French eagle was captured.

ALSO ON THIS DAY

1279

The Crusader Teutonic Knights suffer a heavy defeat at the hands of the Lithuanians at the Battle of Aizkraukle, in present-day Latvia. The Crusaders lost 71 knights, including their grand master.

1426

ENGLAND TRIUMPHANT

The Hundred Years' War was a conflict between England and France waged between 1337 and 1453 (rather more than 100 years) that finally ended any significant involvement of the kings of England in French affairs—though the French would not recapture Calais until 1558.

In the meantime, however, the English won a number of victories on French soil, one being the Battle of St. James in 1426. As the English completed their conquest of northern France, an army commanded by John, Duke of Bedford, regent in France on behalf of England's King Henry VI, defeated the Constable of France, Arthur de Richemont, south of Avranches near the village of Saint-James. As a result, Richemont's brother, Jean V, Duke of Brittany, submitted to England.

> **"King of England, and you, duke of Bedford, who call yourself regent of the kingdom of France... return the keys to all the good towns you took and violated in France."**
>
> —JOAN OF ARC

1814

NAPOLEON OUTGUNNED

> **"May the pens of the diplomats not ruin again what the people have attained with such exertions."**
>
> —GEBHARD VON BLÜCHER

The 1814 campaign in France in many ways showed Napoleon at his finest. The French emperor displayed a mastery of mobile warfare with a paucity of cavalry and mostly inexperienced infantry. But he could not alter one inconvenient fact: his enemies had an overwhelming superiority in the number of experienced infantry and cavalry, which in the end would triumph.

The Battle of Craonne is a case in point. The Prussian marshal Gebhard Leberecht von Blücher had regrouped his army and was advancing on Paris again. Napoleon immediately attacked the combined Prussian and Russian force at Craonne with 37,000 men. Unfortunately for the French, the attack was uncoordinated and their raw conscripts faltered in the face of devastating artillery fire. The Prussians and Russians retreated toward Lâon in what could be considered a narrow French victory.

1722

END OF AN EMPIRE

The Safavid Empire of Iran (Persia) had existed since the dawn of the 14th century, but by the early 1700s was in terminal decline. That decay was highlighted when a Safavid army of up to 50,000 men was defeated by an Afghan army of only 20,000 at the Battle of Gulnabad in 1722. The Afghans were led by Shah Mahmud Hotaki of the Hotaki Dynasty, who after the victory became Shah of Iran. The battle was fought near the city of Isfahan, which Hotaki afterward besieged. It is indicative of the state of the Afghan army that he was forced to starve the city into submission on account of having no artillery with which to force an entrance.

ALSO ON THIS DAY

1965

The first U.S. combat forces arrive on the beaches of Da Nang, Vietnam. They are tasked with protecting the U.S. airbase from Viet Cong attacks.

1862

CLASH OF THE IRONCLADS

Naval history was made at the Battle of Hampton Roads when a Confederate and a Federal ironclad fought each other.

The C.S.S. *Virginia* was a converted frigate equipped with iron plates for protection, armed with six 9-inch (230-mm) guns and four of smaller caliber, and with a complement of 350 men. On March 8 it sailed into Hampton Roads, Virginia, sinking one Union vessel and forcing another aground. The *Virginia* intended to return the next day and finish off the Union fleet, but on March 9 it found the ironclad U.S.S. *Monitor.*

The *Monitor*, armed with two 11-inch (280-mm) guns in a revolving iron turret and with a crew of 58, took up position between the *Virginia* and the crippled Union fleet. For the next few hours, the two ships shot at each other in history's first battle between ironclads. Though the battle was conducted at short range, neither ship's guns could penetrate the armor of the other. The *Monitor* finally withdrew when a shot struck its sight hole, partially blinding the captain, John Lorimer Worden. The Battle of Hampton Roads had illustrated the vulnerability of wooden hulls to armored ships, and ushered in a new era in naval warfare.

1705

THE ROYAL NAVY DEFENDS GIBRALTAR

During the War of the Spanish Succession—a conflict fought to contain Louis XIV of France's ambitions—the French and Spanish laid siege to Gibraltar (recently captured by the British) with land and naval forces.

> **"Virtuous, humane and gallant man, and one of the greatest admirals of his time."**
>
> —DESCRIPTION OF LEAKE BY JOHN CAMPBELL

In February 1705, a French naval squadron of 14 warships and two fireships arrived at Gibraltar, prompting Admiral Sir John Leake to sail from Lisbon with 35 warships to give battle. They arrived off Gibraltar, amid stormy conditions, on March 10. The French ships turned north toward Marbella but were caught by Leake, his ships capturing three French vessels, while two others ran aground. The Battle of Marbella prompted the French to raise the siege of Gibraltar.

1387

DAY OF THE *CONDOTTIERI*

Between the 13th and 16th centuries, many Italian states hired mercenary captains, called *condottieri*, to fight their battles. One of the most famous was the Englishman Sir John Hawkwood. On March 11, 1387, in command of an army representing the city of Padua, he fought the Battle of Castagnaro against the army of the city of Verona. Hawkwood, with 7,000 men-at-arms, 1,000 foot soldiers, and 600 mounted English archers, defeated Giovanni dei Ordelaffi's Veronese army of 9,000 men-at-arms, 2,600 crossbowmen and pikemen, and untrained militia. Hawkwood deployed his men in marshy terrain behind a stream, resisting successive enemy charges before unleashing a cavalry charge that broke the Veronese.

> **"Tell me how you wish me to deal with these enemies of yours, for they are no[t] able to camp, and I will deliver them in your hands in whatever manner you wish."**
>
> —JACOPO DAL VERME IN WILLIAM CAFERRO'S *JOHN HAWKWOOD: AN ENGLISH MERCENARY IN FOURTEENTH-CENTURY ITALY*

MARSHAL NEY KEEPS WELLINGTON AT BAY

In the spring of 1811, during the Peninsular War, France's Marshal Masséna was retreating from the Lines of Torres Vedras: lines of forts constructed in Portugal on the orders of the Duke of Wellington to defend Lisbon. Wellington was pursuing the French at the head of 25,000 troops.

On the morning of March 11, the English advance guard reached the town of Pombal, which was abandoned by the French rearguard under the recklessly brave cavalry commander Marshal Ney. The next day, Ney took up position on the heights near Redinha village, putting himself at the head of his 7,000 troops and determined to keep the English at bay. His men were drawn up in two ranks, supported by artillery and with skirmishers deployed to the fore. His cavalry were placed to the rear.

Wellington assaulted the French position with four divisions, which initially gained the heights but were then thrown back by a French counterattack. The Battle of Redinha continued into the afternoon, Ney defeating all Wellington's attacks before withdrawing across the Ancos River immediately north of the village. He had inflicted 1,800 casualties on the British for the loss of 229 of his own men in a superb example of how to fight a rearguard action. Nevertheless, Marshal Masséna was forced to retreat back into Spain beginning on March 13, bringing to an end his disastrous invasion of Portugal.

▼ Charge of Ney's Division during the Battle of Redinha, Portugal.

1814

THE LAST EMBERS OF GLORY

In March 1814, as the Allies closed in on Paris, Napoleon showed himself still capable of defeating his enemies.

On March 10 he was at Soissons and learned that the Allies had taken Reims, 40 miles (64 km) to the east. With fewer than 30,000 troops, he led a forced march to the city to catch the Prussians and Russians unawares, routing the 13,000 soldiers of General Saint-Priest. Saint-Priest certainly aided the French victory, reacting with lethargy when his advanced troops were driven in, and then taking up a poor position with his main force in front of the city. When he finally realized he was facing the main French Army under Napoleon himself, it was too late. Saint-Priest began to organize a general withdrawal, but was mortally wounded by a cannonball. Napoleon's victory at the Battle of Reims on the 13th recaptured the city and inflicted losses of 6,000 on the enemy. It was to be his last victory of the campaign, however.

As the Allies closed in on Paris, Napoleon showed himself still capable of defeating his enemies.

1590

DECISIVE BATTLE OF THE FRENCH WARS OF RELIGION

The Battle of Ivry was the culmination of eight religious wars that rocked France in the 16th century. The Catholic army commanded by Charles of Lorraine was decisively defeated by the Protestant forces under Henry of Navarre at Ivry, 40 miles (64 km) west of Paris.

Charles had 25,000 men and Henry had only 12,000. But the Protestant forces had more musketeers and better-trained cavalry, and it was a combination of firepower and cavalry attacks that broke the Catholic army, which suffered 4,000 casualties. Protestant losses were only 500. Ironically, three years later Henry converted to Catholicism and became King Henry IV of France.

ALSO ON THIS DAY

1369

Despite support from England, the king of Castille and Leon, Peter the Cruel, is defeated by his half-brother Henry II and his French alliance.

1781

PIVOTAL BATTLE IN AMERICA'S WAR FOR FREEDOM

During the American Revolutionary War, the British Redcoats often proved superior to their American counterparts. But the Americans' battlefield tenacity and courage often resulted in heavy casualties, which sapped the British war effort. This proved the case at the Battle of Guilford Courthouse in 1781.

The Americans' battlefield tenacity and courage often resulted in heavy casualties.

The British Commander in the South, Lieutenant General Charles Cornwallis, scored a tactical victory over American troops commanded by Major General Nathanael Greene at Guilford Courthouse in North Carolina. But he lost a fourth of his 1,900 men in doing so, and had to abandon his campaign for the Carolinas, instead taking his army into Virginia.

▲ American militia firing at the British infantry from behind a split rail fence during the Battle of Guilford Courthouse.

1527

A NEW INDIAN DYNASTY MAKES ITS MARK

The Battle of Khanwa in northern India consolidated the Mughal Empire founded by Babur the year before. Babur's army of just 20,000 troops was faced by a Rajput army of 80,000 men and 500 elephants led by the famed war leader Rana Sanga. But Babur's men had a marked advantage in musketry and artillery, which they employed to good effect during the battle.

The Rajputs attacked the entrenched Mughal positions, resulting in fierce hand-to-hand fighting. Thinking victory was at hand, Rana sent forward his elephants, which were hit by Babur's artillery. Some were killed and the rest panicked, stampeding into Rajput ranks. The Rajput army then dissolved into chaos.

ALSO ON THIS DAY

1322

King Edward II of England defeats rebel barons at the Battle of Boroughbridge, fought northwest of the city of York. The battle is notable for the influence of the longbow on the outcome.

45 BCE

LAST BATTLE OF THE ROMAN CIVIL WAR

Gaius Julius Caesar is one of the great captains of history, a man with a genius for war who was unafraid to grab a sword and lead by example. The Battle of Munda is an instance of his personal courage.

Munda was the final battle between Caesar and the followers of Pompey the Great in Spain. Following the death of Pompey in 48 BCE, his forces were now led by his son, Gnaeus Pompey the Younger. Gnaeus, commanding 13 legions, 6,000 light foot soldiers, and a similar number of Spanish auxiliaries, deployed his army on high ground outside his camp. Caesar, with eight legions and cavalry, deployed his veteran legions on the flanks of his battle line, and personally led his legionaries uphill against the Pompeian forces. The close-quarter combat was unrelenting, but Caesar's 10th legion eventually broke the Pompeian line on the right. At the same time, the cavalry on his left wing also forced the enemy back.

The Pompeians had made a fatal error in committing all their reserves, and had no troops available to stem the Caesarian tide. Soon their whole army was in retreat, which turned into a rout. For the loss of 1,000 men, Caesar inflicted a reported 30,000 losses on the enemy. Gnaeus Pompey was captured and executed.

MARCH 18
1793

A DEFEAT FOR REVOLUTIONARY FRANCE

King Louis XVI was executed in January 1793, prompting an outraged coalition to declare war against France. It consisted of Austria, Sardinia, Britain, Holland, and Spain. But the French National Convention was full of revolutionary fervor, and, far from preparing to defend France, launched offensives against its neighbors to spread the flame of revolution.

General Charles-François Dumouriez, for example, led an attack on Holland, running into an Austro-Dutch army under the command of Archduke Charles of Austria. The subsequent Battle of Neerwinden, fought on March 18, 1793, was a sharp defeat for France, with 3,000 men killed and wounded. Austrian and Dutch losses were 2,600 killed and wounded. Dumouriez was forced to retreat, allowing the Austrians to retake Brussels and drive the French out of what would later become known as Belgium.

> **"The revolution is the war of liberty against its enemies."**
>
> —ROBESPIERRE

MARCH 19
1865

BATTLE OF BENTONVILLE During the American Civil War, General William T. Sherman defeated the Confederate general Joseph Johnston in North Carolina.

MARCH 20
1943

BATTLE OF THE MARETH LINE The British 8th Army's last major set-piece battle in North Africa forced the Axis troops from their last major defensive position in Tunisia.

MARCH 21
1421

BATTLE OF BAUGÉ A Franco-Scottish army of 5,000 defeated English cavalry at the bridge at Baugé during the Hundred Years' War. The Duke of Clarence was killed in the battle.

MARCH 22
871

BATTLE OF MARTON On or about this date, King Æthelred of Wessex and his brother Prince Alfred fought the Vikings in Wiltshire or Dorset, suffering a heavy defeat.

MARCH 23
1862

FIRST BATTLE OF KERNSTOWN Confederate general Jackson is defeated in the first battle of his campaign through Shenandoah Valley by Union colonel Kimball.

MARCH 24
1941

CAPTURE OF EL AGHEILA FORT The German Afrika Korps made their combat debut in North Africa when the 5th Light Division attacked and captured El Agheila Fort.

MARCH 25
1799

FIRST BATTLE OF STOCKACH The Austrian Army defeated the French at Stockach in present-day Baden-Württemberg, Germany, during the Wars of the Second Coalition.

1917

SNATCHING DEFEAT FROM THE JAWS OF VICTORY

Early in 1917, during World War I, the Allies had forced the Turks out of Egypt, allowing British forces to move into Palestine. But before they could do so, they would first have to overcome Turkish defenses situated atop a series of ridges running west to east between the towns of Gaza and Beersheba.

But with the approach of Turkish reinforcements, the ridge was abandoned.

The First Battle of Gaza was the first of three engagements that attempted to overcome those defenses. The attack got off to a promising start, the infantry of the British 53rd Division capturing the Ali Muntar Ridge, unbeknown to headquarters. But with the approach of Turkish reinforcements, the ridge was abandoned. The British lost 4,000 casualties in vain and the defeat encouraged the Turks to defend Gaza more resiliently.

1814

FINAL BATTLE OF THE CREEK WAR

Friction between European settlers and Native Americans often exploded into open hostilities, but the War of 1812 between America and Britain also resulted in civil war between Native peoples.

The Creek peoples occupying what is now Alabama had gathered in a defensive position on the Horseshoe Bend of the Tallapoosa River. On the morning of March 27, 1814, American troops, Tennessee militia, and Cherokee and Creek allies—3,300 men in total—attacked Horseshoe Bend. The defenders numbered 1,000 warriors under Chief Menawa, plus 350 women and children. The attack was directed by General Andrew Jackson and was devastatingly effective, some 800 Creek warriors being killed. The battle ended the Creek War and made Jackson a hero of the American troops and their allies.

The War of 1812 between America and Britain also resulted in civil war between Native peoples.

MUSSOLINI'S PRIDE AND JOY IS DEFEATED

Italian dictator Benito Mussolini dreamed of turning the Mediterranean into an Italian lake—and in early 1941, such a dream appeared not so far-fetched. France had been defeated by Germany, Britain was isolated and on the defensive, and in the Italian Navy Mussolini had a powerful instrument to strike at British ships in the Mediterranean.

On March 26, the Italian Navy launched a major sortie against British convoys sailing to Greece, the Italian squadron including the battleship *Vittorio Veneto*, six heavy cruisers, and 17 destroyers. Unfortunately for the Italians, the British had broken the Axis codes and were alerted to the sortie, dispatching a Royal Navy force comprising three battleships, three light cruisers, 17 destroyers, and an aircraft carrier.

The two fleets clashed at Cape Matapan off the Greek coast on the 28th, British naval gunnery proving devastating. Three Italian heavy cruisers and two destroyers were sunk, the battleship and one destroyer being damaged. Over 2,000 Italian sailors lost their lives compared to three British fatalities. Four British ships were lightly damaged.

The Battle of Cape Matapan was Italy's greatest defeat at sea during World War II, and its navy has never truly recovered from it.

▼ Practice session on an Italian battleship in the Mediterranean Sea, before Italy's defeat a year later. Photograph taken in June 1940.

1461

ONE OF THE BLOODIEST BATTLES ON ENGLISH SOIL

The Battle of Towton, during the Wars of the Roses, resulted in 28,000 men dying in combat.

To enforce his claim to the English throne, the Yorkist King Edward IV marched an army north to attack the Lancastrian army of King Henry VI and Queen Margaret. The armies, each around 30,000-strong, met in a snowstorm on an open field between the villages of Towton and Saxton in North Yorkshire.

The Lancastrians occupied a strong position on a slope, their flank secured by Cock Creek. But the Yorkists had the wind at their backs, which allowed their archers to shoot and hit the Lancastrians without the latter being able to reply. Goaded into action, the Lancastrians left their positions to get to grips with the enemy. For the next six hours a furious hand-to-hand battle waged, until fresh Yorkist troops smashed into the Lancastrian flank. Henry's men broke and fled, hundreds of armored knights drowning while trying to ford the creek, and thousands more being cut down by Yorkists.

King Henry, Queen Margaret, and their son escaped to Scotland. But after Towton, the Lancastrians would be unable to raise an army for another three years.

It is difficult to estimate casualties, but from contemporary accounts it is possible to come to a figure of around 28,000, of which 20,000 were Lancastrians.

▼ Lord Fauconbridge at the Battle of Towton, during the English Wars of the Roses.

MARCH 30

1814

THE FALL OF NAPOLEON

At the end of March 1814, four huge Allied columns, under the command of the Austrian field marshal Prince Karl von Schwarzenberg, converged on Paris. Napoleon had given the task of strengthening the city's defenses to his older brother Joseph, who proved signally incompetent in doing so. He was reinforced by the arrival of Marshal Auguste de Marmont with 3,000 soldiers, to which were added 20,000 regulars and 6,000 National Guardsmen. Approaching the city were 155,000 Allied soldiers.

The Battle of Paris on March 30 had a foreseeable outcome. The Allies struck the eastern outskirts of the city before dawn, Joseph fled before noon, and the city was abandoned just after midnight. Its fall would lead to Napoleon's abdication.

ALSO ON THIS DAY

1916

On the Eastern Front in World War I, the Russian Lake Naroch Offensive is called off. It began on March 18 but has failed to break through strong German defenses. Russian casualties are 110,000.

MARCH 31

1865

COSTLY UNION VICTORY AT WHITE OAK ROAD

In March 1865, during the American Civil War, Union general Ulysses S. Grant was trying to outflank Confederate defenses at Petersburg to cut the Southside Railroad, the last Confederate supply line.

Grant sent Major General Warren's V Corps, plus Brigadier General Nelson Miles' division of II Corps—22,000 men in total—to cut the supply line. They ran into 8,000 Confederate troops, commanded by Major General Richard Anderson, 11 miles (17.6 km) southwest of Petersburg in woods between White Oak Road and Boydton Plank Road. The resulting Battle of White Oak Road was a Union victory costing 1,870 casualties. Confederate losses were 800, which they could ill afford.

ALSO ON THIS DAY

1865

The Battle of Dinwiddie Court House, fought during the American Civil War and part of the Appomattox Campaign, resulted in a Confederate victory, with some 65,000 troops involved.

CHAPTER 4
April

A NAIL IN PETERSBURG'S COFFIN

The Union victory at White Oak Road on March 31 threatened the besieged city of Petersburg's last supply line, prompting Confederate general Robert E. Lee to send Major General George Pickett with one infantry division and two cavalry divisions to hold the vital crossroads of Five Forks, 5 miles (8 km) west of the previous day's fighting.

Some 10,000 Confederate troops began constructing fieldworks, but these proved inadequate when 22,000 Union troops under the command of Major Generals Philip Sheridan and Gouverneur Warren attacked on the afternoon of April 1. Pickett was actually absent from the battlefield, having lunch. The Confederate left flank was speedily overwhelmed, with the loss of many prisoners. The last part of the Confederate line to collapse was the center at the road junction, which was held by artillery until overrun by Federal cavalry.

The Battle of Five Forks cost the Confederates 2,950 men, most of them captured, compared to Union losses of 830. But, more importantly, it meant that Lee could no longer secure his last supply line into Petersburg: the Southside Railroad. The next day, Lee informed President Davis that Petersburg and the Confederate capital, Richmond, must be evacuated.

▼ Confederate prisoners under guard in the U.S. on April 2, 1865. The prisoners were captured during the American Civil War battle of Five Forks, Virginia, by Union Army general Sherman.

1801

THE NELSON TOUCH

Horatio Nelson was one of Britain's great naval heroes, who in the early 1800s won a series of victories that gave the Royal Navy command of the seas. The Battle of Copenhagen in 1801 was one of those victories.

Britain was on the defensive in 1800 in the face of French aggression. And to add to its woes, the neutral nations of Russia, Prussia, Sweden, and Denmark formed the Northern Convention to resist British rights in the Baltic.

On April 2, 1801, Admiral Sir Hyde Parker sailed a fleet of 20 warships into Copenhagen harbor, Denmark, to deliver an ultimatum to Crown Prince Frederick. The Danes opened fire with shore batteries. Parker ordered his ships to withdraw but his second-in-command, Admiral Nelson, ignored the signal and led the ships into the attack. After first silencing the shore batteries with broadsides, the British ships then turned their attention on the ten Danish vessels anchored in the harbor. Raked with broadsides, all ten were disabled. The Danes accepted a truce on April 3. British casualties were 253 killed and 688 wounded. The Danes losses were 790 killed, 900 wounded, and 2,000 taken prisoner.

▲ The Battle of Copenhagen during the Napoleonic Wars, Denmark.

1367

CIVIL WAR IN SPAIN BETWEEN TWO BROTHERS

When King Alfonso of Castile died in 1350 he was succeeded by his son Peter, but after 16 years of rule, his crown was challenged by his half-brother Henry, who had the support of the French. The resulting civil war became part of the Hundred Years' War when Peter fled to English-controlled territory in France and petitioned Edward, the Black Prince, for aid, which he received. Peter and the Black Prince marched back to Spain where they defeated Henry's army at the Battle of Navarrete (or Nájera) on this day. But Henry escaped to fight another day and would eventually become King of Castile.

ALSO ON THIS DAY

1898

Spanish forces defeat Filipino rebels at the Battle of Tres de Abril during the Philippine Revolution. The battle is fought in the city of Cebu.

2004

TOUGH BATTLE FOR FALLUJAH

The First Battle of Fallujah was an attempt to rid the Iraqi city of insurgents and extremists. U.S. forces comprising Marines, U.S. Army units, and Special Forces personnel, totaling 2,000 troops, immediately encountered heavy small-arms fire and rocket attacks, and despite U.S. firepower and air support, by April 9 the city remained under insurgent control.

Fallujah was a nightmare for U.S. forces, with narrow streets lined by walls and houses built close together, allowing insurgents to lie hidden until they opened fire with small arms and rocket-propelled grenades, plus hand grenades. In addition, the insurgents converted houses into fortified fighting positions.

After three weeks and six days of heavy fighting, during which 28 Americans were killed, U.S. forces withdrew from Fallujah and handed over control to the CIA-trained Fallujah Brigade, which promptly deserted and joined the insurgency.

The First Battle of Fallujah was an attempt to rid the Iraqi city of insurgents and extremists.

1242

BATTLE ON THE ICE

Sergei Eisenstein's 1938 film *Alexander Nevsky* immortalized the Battle of Lake Peipus.

Alexander, Prince of the Russian city of Novgorod, responded to an invasion of his homeland by 2,600 German Teutonic Knights, led by Bishop Hermann of Dorpat, by raising an army of 5,000. The two forces met on the ice of the frozen lake. The German knights, mostly former members of the Catholic order of the Brothers of the Sword, formed into a wedge and charged at the Russian center, which buckled. But the Danes and Estonians on the flanks were assaulted by Russian cavalry and mounted archers, and were soon fleeing, leaving the knights surrounded. Defeat followed, and Novgorod remained in Russian hands.

The two forces met on the ice of the frozen lake. The German knights formed into a wedge and charged at the Russian center, which buckled.

46 BCE

CAESAR'S AFRICAN TRIUMPH

Caesar formed his army into three lines and deployed missile troops to panic the elephants, which disrupted the Pompeian battle line.

The Battle of Thapsus ended the second Roman Civil War.

While Julius Caesar was besieging the city of Thapsus (in present-day Tunisia), Metellus Scipio, a supporter of the late Pompey the Great, approached with a relief force, whereupon Caesar marched out to meet him. Scipio had 86,000 soldiers and 64 war elephants, Caesar's army being smaller at 55,000. Forming his army into three lines, he deployed missile troops to panic the elephants, which disrupted the Pompeian battle line. Caesar then launched his legionaries to break Scipio's army. Caesar suffered around 1,000 casualties, Scipio ten times as many. This victory led to the capture or suicide of many prominent republicans.

END OF AN ERA IN NAVAL WARFARE

▲ A photograph of the IJN *Yamato*, the lead ship of the *Yamato* class of battleships that served with the Imperial Japanese Navy during World War II.

The Japanese battleship *Yamato* was the biggest warship ever built, armed with 150 guns of various calibers and protected by thick armor. In April 1945, it and nine other ships were steaming toward the U.S. fleet off the embattled island of Okinawa, aiming to sink the American warships and save the island. But the age of the battleship was over.

Shortly after noon on the 7th, U.S. carrier aircraft attacked the *Yamato*. A bomb from a Helldiver destroyed a gun turret, killing all five crew. Meanwhile, Corsair and Hellcat fighters were raking her decks with machine-gun fire, and Avenger torpedo-bombers were releasing their ordnance. Three torpedoes struck the *Yamato*'s hull and exploded, causing the ship to list. Another slammed into the ship's stern, jamming its main rudder. The ship was now locked in a counterclockwise turn from which there was no escape.

At 14:23 hours, the *Yamato* exploded, sending a massive plume of black smoke a mile (1.6 km) into the sky. The explosion sent thousands of shrapnel fragments into the air, killing all the Japanese sailors in the water who had managed to get off the *Yamato*. The battleship's end signaled that the Imperial Japanese Navy had ceased to exist.

1864

REBEL YELL IN LOUISIANA

By the fourth year of the American Civil War, the Union was in the ascendancy—but the Confederates could still win the odd victory if well led. A case in point was the Battle of Mansfield, fought this day in Louisiana.

General Grant's Red River Campaign, designed to bring pressure on Confederate armies along five separate fronts between Louisiana and Virginia, resulted in General Banks' 12,000 Union soldiers threatening Shreveport, Louisiana. In response, Confederate general Taylor, seeking to delay the enemy, established a defensive position at Mansfield with 9,000 men. After a desultory Union assault, Taylor counterattacked, inflicting 2,000 casualties on the enemy for the loss of 1,000 Confederates. This defeat prompted Banks to begin an overall retreat.

Confederate general Taylor, seeking to delay the enemy, established a defensive position at Mansfield with 9,000 men.

1241

THE UNSTOPPABLE MONGOLS

The Mongol invasion of Europe was terrifying and unstoppable. The Mongol army of Kaidu, a grandson of Genghis Khan, slammed into a Christian army under the command of Henry II, Duke of Silesia, at the Battle of Liegnitz (now Legnica in Poland).

The Christian knights, including Teutonic Knights, and Silesian foot soldiers were lured forward by a feigned retreat of the Mongols' mounted archers, whereupon the heavy Mongol cavalry attacked the knights on the flanks and from behind. Duke Henry and his knights were slaughtered, as were most of the 20,000 men he had brought to the battlefield. Losses to the Mongol army are unknown.

ALSO ON THIS DAY

1782

The British navy achieves a decisive victory over the French at the Battle of Dominica in the Caribbean.

1741

TRIUMPH OF THE IRON RAMROD

Often the smallest things can make a difference in battle. On this day, 21,000 Prussian soldiers led by Frederick the Great fought Field Marshal von Neipperg's 19,000 Austrians at the Battle of Mollwitz, Silesia. The Austrians routed the Prussian horsemen on the right and then turned on the Prussian infantry. Five times the Austrian horse charged, being repulsed each time by accurate musket fire. Then the Prussian infantry advanced, firing at twice the rate of the Austrians because they had iron ramrods, as opposed to the wooden ones in general use at the time. The result was a decisive Prussian victory, the Austrians suffering 5,000 dead, wounded, and captured.

ALSO ON THIS DAY

1863

Union forces defeat Confederate troops of the 1st Cavalry Corps at the Battle of Franklin, Tennessee, during the American Civil War. Confederate losses are 137; Union casualties total 100.

1544

THE VALLEY OF DEATH

At the Battle of Ceresole, in the Piedmont region of Italy, the cost of close-quarter combat in the pike and shot era was brutally illustrated. A French army of 11,000 infantry and 1,800 cavalry, commanded by the Count of Enghien, fought troops from Spain and the Holy Roman Empire amounting to 12,500 foot and 1,000 cavalry. Both sides deployed their forces on the crests of ridges, after which came a four-hour skirmish between arquebusiers that achieved very little. But when the infantry, comprising pikemen and arquebusiers of both armies, descended into the valley, the result was a blood-bath. The French side eventually prevailed, inflicting more than 6,000 deaths on the enemy and capturing 3,000 more.

The battle achieved very little, since the Spanish still occupied most of the fortresses in Lombardy. However, Enghien did capture Alessandria later in the year. Following his success in Italy, Enghien was made governor of Languedoc and a promising military career beckoned. However, he was killed in an accident in 1546, aged 27.

APRIL 12 2003

OPERATION IRAQI FREEDOM

The U.S. 3rd Infantry Division was the unit spearheading the drive on Baghdad, launching its first so-called "thunder run" —a fast, armored strike into the city—on April 5, and the second two days later.

It was on April 12 that the Iraqi capital, Baghdad, was captured as part of Operation Iraqi Freedom, the U.S.-led offensive to remove Saddam Hussein from power. United States forces had surrounded Baghdad on April 6, and the next day tanks began to advance into the city. By April 8, coalition forces were moving around at will inside Baghdad, Saddam Hussain having fled the city. Pockets of resistance remained, however, and the breakdown of law and order led to widespread looting on April 9. On April 12, Baghdad having been secured, divisions of the U.S. I Marine Expeditionary Force left Baghdad to head for Saddam's home city of Tikrit.

Baghdad was captured as part of Operation Iraqi Freedom, the U.S.-led offensive to remove Saddam Hussein from power.

APRIL 13 1777

RATTLING THE CONTINENTALS

"I was ordered to form the advanced guard of General Grant's column. At daybreak, I came upon an enemy picket on this side of the stone causeway which led to Bound Brook through a marsh."

—HESSIAN CAPTAIN JOHANN EWALD

In the spring of 1777, during the American Revolutionary War, the British decided to make a surprise attack against the American fort at Bound Brook on the Raritan River, New Jersey. A force of 4,000 British and Hessian troops, commanded by General Charles Cornwallis, arrived at the fort late on April 13, launching an attack the next morning. The American defenders, 500 men under the command of Major General Benjamin Lincoln, managed to evacuate the fort via an unblocked route, though not before losing 40 killed, 40 wounded, and 80 captured. British losses at the Battle of Bound Brook were just one killed and seven wounded.

1471

DEATH OF THE KINGMAKER

The Battle of Barnet did not end the Wars of the Roses, but it was hugely significant, for it cost the life of Richard Neville, Earl of Warwick, known as "the Kingmaker."

The Yorkist King Edward IV returned from exile in Burgundy and landed in Yorkshire with a few mercenaries. Dashing south, he established himself in London and built up an army of 10,000 men. Warwick, caught off guard, marched down from the north with the same number of men, making camp opposite Edward at Barnet, north of London, on the night of April 13. The 14th dawned foggy, and the two armies found themselves misaligned against each other. In the confusing battle that followed, the Earl of Oxford and his men, fighting for Warwick, were shot at by friendly archers who mistook the earl's Rising Sun badge for Edward's Sun with Streams. At this, Oxford's men cried foul and fled the battlefield. Edward chose this moment to advance, striking the center of the Lancastrian army and breaking Warwick's men.

The Kingmaker tried to flee but was overtaken and cut down, dying along with 1,000 of his men. Yorkist losses were 500.

▼ An illustration of the death of Richard Neville, Earl of Warwick and "the Kingmaker," at the Battle of Barnet, killed by troops of Edward IV.

The Battle of Barnet cost the life of Richard Neville, Earl of Warwick, known as "the Kingmaker."

1450

ECLIPSE OF THE LONGBOW

The longbow had won the English some great victories during the Hundred Years' War. But by the middle of the 15th century, gunpowder was beginning to eclipse the bowmen of England.

At the Battle of Formigny, 5,000 Englishmen commanded by Thomas Kyriell were defeated by a similar number of Frenchmen. The French were careful to remain beyond the range of the longbows, launching one infantry and two cavalry attacks, all of which were repulsed. The French commander, the Comte de Clermont, then brought forward his two cannons, which began firing at the English. The English sallied forth and captured the cannon, but the sound of artillery had alerted some nearby French cavalry, 1,200 horsemen under Constable de Richemont appearing in the English rear. Kyriell attempted to redeploy his men to meet both threats, but when the two French groups attacked simultaneously his army disintegrated into small groups, which were systematically surrounded and destroyed. The French killed nearly 4,000 Englishmen for the loss of 200.

This decisive battle ended the fighting in northern France. Normandy quickly reverted to French control and by 1453 only Calais remained in English hands.

1746

THE CRUSHING OF THE CLANS

The last major battle fought on British soil took place on Drummossie Moor, overlooking the Scottish city of Inverness. The Battle of Culloden was the final act of the Jacobite Rebellion of Charles Edward Stewart against the British king George II.

Having failed to incite rebellion in England, Charles withdrew back to Scotland with 6,000 men until he reached Inverness. He was pursued by a British army of 8,000 men under the command of the Duke of Cumberland. Ignoring advice to the contrary, Charles decided to fight Cumberland on Drummossie Moor, despite the ground being marshy, which would inhibit his Highlanders' best tactic: their frontal charge.

Accepting battle, Cumberland's artillery pounded the Scots for half an hour with roundshot and grapeshot. Charles then unleashed his Highlanders who, despite the boggy ground, reached the Redcoats. But the latter had been trained to attack the enemy to their right with their bayonets, instead of the one to the front (the Highlanders usually carried a shield on their left side). After less than half an hour, the Scots broke and fled, leaving up to 2,000 dead on the battlefield. British losses were 300.

APRIL 17

1918

BELGIAN HEROISM IN THE TRENCHES

In World War I, the Belgian Army defended its homeland stoutly in the face of overwhelming German might.

In April 1918, the German Army launched an offensive to break through Belgian lines north of Ypres and take the French port of Dunkirk (Dunkerque). Standing in its way were the Belgians, who had prepared defenses in depth to resist any attacks. And at the Battle of Merkem, fought on this day, they threw back a German attack to the southwest and north of Ypres in the Belgian Army's first victory of the war. The culmination of the battle occurred when the 3rd Royal Division launched a bayonet attack that captured 800 prisoners.

▼ Infantry soldiers charge the Germans at Merkem, Flanders, Belgium.

APRIL 18

1847

THE DRIVE TO MEXICO CITY

During the Mexican–American War of 1846–8, U.S. general Winfield Scott was advancing toward the Mexican capital. To block his advance, Mexican general Santa Anna occupied the strategic mountain pass of Cerro Gordo with 12,000 troops. Scott's 10,000 troops arrived on April 12, and a reconnaissance concluded that a frontal assault would be costly.

However, a Captain Robert E. Lee (the future Confederate commander) found a route around Santa Anna's left flank, which was used by 7,000 U.S. troops under General David Twiggs to strike at the Mexicans' camp. Fearing encirclement, Santa Anna fled, leaving 1,000 dead and 3,000 prisoners behind. U.S. losses at the Battle of Cerro Gordo were 400.

To block U.S. general Winfield Scott's advance, Mexican general Santa Anna occupied the strategic mountain pass of Cerro Gordo with 12,000 troops.

THE FIRST SHOTS OF FREEDOM

Tension between the British Crown and its American colonies finally erupted into war in 1775. To preempt any violence, the British general Thomas Gage sent Colonel Francis Smith with 800 troops to seize weapons and powder at Concord, Massachusetts. He arrived at the small town of Lexington at 05:00 hours on the morning of April 19. Barring his way was a small militia force of 70 under the command of Captain John Parker.

It remains uncertain who fired the first shot, but the British responded with a volley that killed seven militiamen, the rest fleeing. Smith moved on to Concord, reaching North Bridge where a force of 400 militiamen stood on the high ground across the river. The militia advanced, whereupon the British retreated back across the bridge, a brief skirmish ensuing. Smith then decided to retreat back to Boston. This turned into a rout as the Redcoats were harried along their route by American fire.

Having heard of the battle at Lexington, Gage sent troops that linked up with Smith's retreating force near Lexington. The combined force of Redcoats was harassed by the Americans until it reached Boston at 20:00 hours. They had lost 73 men, and many more wounded, in the first battle of the American Revolutionary War.

▼ A print by John H. Daniels and Sons, Boston, showing the first shots of the American War of Independence at the Battle of Lexington.

1657

A BLACK DAY FOR THE SPANISH NAVY

During the Anglo-Spanish War of 1654–60, one of the English objectives was to seize Spanish bullion transported across the Atlantic from the Americas. In 1656, Admiral Robert Blake set sail with 23 ships to do just that, intercepting a Spanish bullion fleet off Tenerife in the Canary Islands.

On April 20, 1657, Blake attacked the Spanish fleet and shore batteries in Santa Cruz harbor in the Battle of Santa Cruz de Tenerife. Due to faulty dispositions, the second line of Spanish ships shielded the English ships from those batteries, allowing Blake's ships to destroy 16 Spanish vessels (the silver bullion had been taken ashore) for no loss to his own fleet, though one ship was badly damaged.

One of the English objectives was to seize Spanish bullion transported across the Atlantic from the Americas.

1703

SWEDISH TRIUMPH AT PUŁTUSK

When the Swedes attacked, the Saxon commander, Field Marshal Steinau, ordered a retreat into the town.

The Great Northern War (1700–21) was fought between Sweden and a coalition that desired to cripple Swedish power in the Baltic. One member of that coalition, Saxony, was defeated by Charles XII of Sweden in 1702. The following spring, Charles struck north from Kraków to search for the Saxon army again, finding it at Pułtusk, 32 miles (51 km) north of Warsaw, on April 21.

The 10,000 Saxons were deployed on a ridge west of the town, but when the Swedes attacked, the Saxon commander, Field Marshal Steinau, ordered a retreat into the town. However, Swedish cavalry attacked and got into the town, inflicting casualties and taking prisoners. Some 600 Saxons were killed in the defeat and 1,000 captured. The Swedes lost 21 men.

DAVOUT—MILITARY GENIUS

Napoleon was fortunate to have so many gifted generals under his command, none more so than Louis-Nicolas Davout. The French marshal demonstrated his abilites during the Battle of Eckmühl, in Bavaria.

Due to a miscalculation on the part of Napoleon, the bulk of his army was deployed against the left wing of the Austrian Army. This left Marshal Davout with 20,000 men to face 75,000 Austrians at Eckmühl, 23 miles (37 km) from the main body.

The Austrian commander, Archduke Charles, launched an attack intending to turn the French left flank along the Danube, and by 13:00 was in the process of overwhelming the French despite Davout's leadership. A courier arrived with news that French reinforcements under Marshal Lannes were on their way. Davout therefore launched a counterattack to buy time. The fighting was savage but allowed for Lannes' 30,000 troops to arrive and win the battle. With both his flanks smashed and his army exhausted, Archduke Charles ordered a retreat. He had suffered 7,000 casualties and 5,000 men captured. French losses were also high at 6,000 casualties, but Davout had won a hard-fought victory against heavy odds, and was afterward made Prince of Eckmühl by a grateful French emperor. Most of Eckmühl's army managed to escape across the River Danube, though Napoleon was able to capture Vienna immediately afterwards.

▼ Napoleon leads his army during the Battle of Eckmühl, in Bavaria.

APRIL 23 1809

WINNING THE KEY TO VIENNA

After Davout's victory at Eckmühl, Napoleon pursued the Austrian Army but found his path blocked by the garrison of Ratisbon (now Regensburg), a city at the confluence of the Danube, Naab, and Regen rivers. Eager to take the city, Napoleon ordered Marshal Lannes to storm it on the 23rd.

Napoleon sited artillery and began a bombardment of the southeast corner of the city's walls. During this bombardment, he suffered a minor wound when a spent bullet grazed his foot. Although the bullet did not break his skin, news soon spread that the emperor had been injured, lowering morale. As a result, Napoleon was forced to tour his units to reassure his men he was unhurt.

The French soldiers were losing heart and refusing to mount a third assault after two attacks failed with heavy losses, which led the marshal to grab a ladder and declare his intention to attack on his own. At this, the shamefaced soldiers raced forward, stormed the defenses, and within minutes were inside the city.They had suffered 2,000 casualties, but victory at the Battle of Ratisbon left Napoleon free to advance on Vienna.

APRIL 24 1862

NEW ORLEANS BREACHED The attack by a Union naval squadron led New Orleans to surrender on April 25 in a major Confederacy disaster in the American Civil War.

APRIL 25 1626

VICTORY FOR IMPERIAL GERMAN CATHOLIC FORCES The victory over a Danish Protestant army at Dessau Bridge came during the Thirty Years' War (1618–48).

APRIL 26 1794

BATTLE OF BEAUMONT An Anglo-Austrian army defeated a French army attempting to relieve the besieged fortress of Landrecies during the War of the First Coalition.

APRIL 27 1799

FRENCH SUFFER DEFEAT During the War of the Second Coalition, Alexander Suvorov's Austro-Russian army defeated Jean Moreau's French army at Cassano in northern Italy.

APRIL 28 1758

CLASH OF THE EMPIRES The Indian Maratha win a decisive victory after they clashed with the Afghan Durrani empires at Attock (near present-day Islamabad, Pakistan).

APRIL 29 1781

FOUR-HOUR NAVAL BATTLE The larger French fleet forced the British to retire in a battle fought off Fort Royal on Martinique (West Indies) in the Anglo-French War.

APRIL 30 1904

BATTLE BY THE YALU RIVER The first major land battle of the Russo-Japanese War took place on the border between Korea and China. The Japanese are victorious.

CHAPTER
5
May

MAY 1 1690

THE LAST JACOBITE BATTLE

The Catholic King James II of England had fled to Ireland to continue his war against William III, sending aid when he could to the Jacobites, his supporters in Scotland. In 1690, he sent Major General Buchan to Scotland to command the Jacobites. But his Highland allies were at a low ebb, having just been defeated at the Battle of Dunkeld the previous year. At a meeting with the chiefs, Buchan was told the Highlanders would continue the war, but not until their springtime tasks had been completed. This left Buchan with an army of around 1,200 men, which he intended to use to attack the enemy's quarters along the borders of the lowlands.

He got as far as Cromdale in Inverness-shire, where he camped on April 30, 1690, his numbers having dwindled to 800. The next day, he was attacked by a larger government force under the command of Sir Thomas Livingstone. When Livingstone's men appeared on the other side of the Spey River, the Jacobites began to retreat, but the government cavalry crossed the river and intercepted them. In the subsequent Battle of Cromdale, 400 Jacobites were killed for the loss of 100 government troops. This battle ended the Jacobite Rebellion in Scotland.

▼ The Earl of Angus' regiment (the Cameronians) at the Defense of Dunkeld.

MAY

1945

CAPTURING THE "LAIR OF THE FASCIST BEAST"

The Battle of Berlin came to an end on May 2, when General Helmuth Weidling, commander of the city garrison, surrendered to the Red Army.

The Red Army's Berlin Offensive had begun on April 16, 2.5 million troops, 41,000 artillery pieces, 6,200 tanks and assault guns, and 7,200 aircraft striking toward Hitler's capital. As the Russian troops battled their way into the city, Hitler committed suicide on April 30, the Soviets capturing the shot-pummeled Reichstag the day after. By the time the city surrendered on May 2, the Red Army had losses of 81,000 killed and 272,000 wounded. German casualties are estimated at around 500,000 killed and captured. The battle signaled the end of World War II in Europe, though fighting would continue for a few more days.

The Battle of Berlin came to an end on May 2, when General Helmuth Weidling, commander of the city garrison, surrendered to the Red Army.

MAY

1815

MARSHAL MURAT'S WATERLOO

The flamboyant French cavalry commander, Joachim Murat, had been one of Napoleon's marshals, the emperor making him King of Naples in 1808. He deserted Napoleon in 1813 but supported him again in 1815. This brought him into conflict with the Austrians, who sent two corps to topple him.

Murat engaged the Austrians at the two-day battle of Tolentino, southern Italy, which concluded on May 3. Murat was defeated and the Neapolitan Army ceased to exist as a cohesive fighting force. Murat fled to Corsica, only to return to try to retake his crown. He failed and was executed in October 1815.

ALSO ON THIS DAY

1942

Japanese troops invade Tulagi Island in the Solomons, during World War II, during the first phase of Operation Mo—their plan to capture New Guinea from the Australians.

MAY

1471

YORKIST TRIUMPH AT TEWKESBURY

Following his victory at the Battle of Barnet, the Yorkist King Edward IV moved swiftly west to confront a Lancastrian army led by Queen Margaret, wife of Henry VI. The two armies met at the Battle of Tewkesbury. The 7,000 Lancastrians took up a strong position on a slope behind a stream, and the Duke of Somerset mounted a flanking attack against Edward's 6,000 troops. The flanking move almost worked, but Somerset was eventually driven back and then ambushed by 200 spearmen. The Yorkists then attacked the Lancastrian center where Henry's son, Prince Edward, was killed. After that, the entire Lancastrian army fell apart. Edward's throne was never seriously challenged again.

ALSO ON THIS DAY

1799

British troops storm the fortress of Seringapatam, India, to bring the war between the British East India Company and the Kingdom of Mysore to an end.

MAY

1811

WELLINGTON'S INVASION OF SPAIN

Following the retreat of the French Army from the Lisbon area in the spring of 1811, the Duke of Wellington launched a two-pronged invasion of Spain. He led one column with 30,000 British and Portuguese troops, marching eastward to Almeida near the Spanish border and laying siege to the town.

In response, Marshal André Masséna set out from Ciudad Rodrigo with 30,000 soldiers to raise the siege. Wellington took up a strong position at Fuentes de Oñoro, 10 miles (16 km) to the south of Almeida. In the ensuing battle of Fuentes de Oñoro, Masséna was defeated and fell back to his base after suffering 2,000 losses. Wellington sustained 1,500 casualties but was able to seize Almeida.

Following the retreat of the French Army from the Lisbon area in the spring of 1811, the Duke of Wellington launched a two-pronged invasion of Spain.

MAY

53 BCE

A BLIZZARD OF ARROWS AT CARRHAE

In 53 BCE, one of Rome's Triumvirate, Marcus Licinius Crassus, invaded the Parthian Empire at the head of 50,000 troops, of which 42,000 were legionaries. The rest were 4,000 cavalry and 4,000 light infantry. The Romans regarded the Parthians as effete easterners who would easily succumb to Rome's legions. The Battle of Carrhae, near Haran in modern Turkey, would shock the Roman world.

The Parthian force that rode to intercept Crassus was heavily outnumbered, being composed of 9,000 mounted archers and 1,000 cataphracts (rider and horse encased in armor). But the Parthian commander, Surena, also had a camel train of arrows to replenish his horse archers when battle commenced.

Crassus formed up his army in a great square to resist the Parthian horsemen, which began showering the legionaries with arrows. When the Romans charged the Parthians, the mounted archers retreated speedily, shooting over the hind quarters of their horses as they did so (the famous "Parthian shot"). Crassus' son Publius headed a charge and both he and his men were surrounded and killed.

Having a seemingly inexhaustible supply of arrows, the Parthians wore down the Roman Army, which began a disorderly retreat. Crassus' losses were 20,000 men killed and a further 10,000 captured at Carrhae, Crassus himself being killed a few days later by the Parthians.

Crassus at the Battle of Carrhae.

MAY

1954

FRENCH DISASTER AT DIEN BIEN PHU

In 1953, the French High Command in Indochina, losing a war against the Viet Minh guerrillas, decided to force a battle on the plain of Dien Bien Phu on the border of Laos and Vietnam. The result would be disastrous.

The French base was defended by 10,800 men, with artillery, tanks, and aircraft, but the Viet Minh under the command of General Vo Nguyen Giap massed 37,500 troops and artillery around the base. On March 13, 1954, the Viet Minh attacked, reducing the base's outlying strongholds one by one. By March 15, Giap had captured the strategic ridges to the north and northeast of the base and could use his artillery to pound Dien Bien Phu at will. Two days later, his army had grown to 40,000 men and his guns began striking the base's airstrip. By March 23, all flights in and out of the base had been halted by Viet Minh artillery. For the rest of the siege, the French were supplied by parachute (though only at night, as the flak during daylight hours was too heavy).

By the afternoon of May 7, it was all over. Defeat at Dien Bien Phu shocked the French public and political opinion, and would lead to France agreeing to the independence of Vietnam. The garrison had suffered 4,000 dead, the rest being led into captivity. Giap had 8,000 dead and 15,000 wounded soldiers.

▼ French paratroopers arrive in Dien Bien Phu, Indochina.

MAY

1429

JOAN OF ARC TURNS THE TIDE IN THE HUNDRED YEARS' WAR

The English had been besieging the city of Orléans in central France since October 1428, constructing a number of siege forts around the city. French morale was low after a number of defeats, but the arrival of the peasant girl Joan of Arc reinvigorated French forces. Supposedly on a devout mission on the orders of God, she was soon leading French troops to success, capturing the English siege-fort of Saint-Loup on May 4; on May 7 she led an attack on the English that killed 300 and captured a further 200. On May 8, the English abandoned their positions and marched away from Orléans. The Battle of Orléans marked a turning point in the Hundred Years' War.

Following her victory at Orléans, Joan tried to take Paris but failed. She was captured in May 1430 by the Burgundians and handed over to the English, who burned her at the stake in Rouen on May 30, 1431.

The arrival of the peasant girl Joan of Arc reinvigorated French forces.

MAY

1645

MONTROSE: SCOTLAND'S BRAVE CAVALIER

James Graham, Marquis of Montrose, was a brilliant Cavalier commander during the English Civil War, who led a ragtag army of Highland clansmen and Irish foot soldiers to a series of stunning victories over the better-equipped and larger armies of the Scottish Covenant (an influential Presbyterian organization).

James Graham led a ragtag army of Highland clansmen and Irish foot soldiers to a series of stunning victories.

One such victory was won at the Battle of Auldearn, east of Nairn. The 3,900 Covenanters outnumbered the Royalist army of 1,550, but Montrose hid most of his army in a hollow, waiting until the Covenanters had advanced against what they believed to be his main force, before unleashing the bulk of his forces in a flank attack. The result was a Covenant rout in which 1,500 were killed.

MAY 10 1796

A WOODEN BRIDGE AT LODI

The Battle of the bridge of Lodi was an insignificant action during the French Revolutionary Wars. But it increased the aura of a young French general named Napoleon Bonaparte, who was achieving famous victories during his first Italian campaign and laying the foundations of his own meteoric rise.

After knocking Sardinia out of the war, Napoleon turned his attention to the Austrian Army of General Baron de Beaulieu (24,000 men), which fell back across the Adda River. This left the road to Milan open, but Napoleon wanted to secure his right flank. He entered Lodi on this day, establishing a battery to pound Austrian defenses across the Adda. He then sent infantry across the 200-yard (185-meter) wooden bridge over the river. The troops were raked by enemy cannon and musket fire, but such was the élan of the French troops that despite suffering 400 casualties, they reached the far bank and bayoneted the Austrian troops surrounding the cannon. Shaken by the attack, Beaulieu beat a hasty retreat toward Mantua. Each side suffered 2,000 casualties during the battle, but Napoleon had won another victory and later entered Milan like a conquering Caesar. The Bonaparte legend was growing.

Napoleon wrote after the battle: "It was only on the evening of Lodi that I believed myself a superior man."

▲ General Bonaparte giving orders at the Battle of Lodi.

MAY

11

1864

DEATH OF A CONFEDERATE CAVALIER

In 1864, during the American Civil War, Major General Philip H. Sheridan was in command of the Union Army's Cavalry Corps. On May 9, Sheridan took his 10,000 cavalrymen south with orders to defeat his Confederate counterpart, J. E. B. Stuart, disrupt Rebel supply lines, and threaten Richmond, Virginia. The two cavalry forces clashed on this day at the Battle of Yellow Tavern, Stuart mustering 4,500 horsemen. In a swirling battle, Sheridan forced the Confederates to retire, Stuart having received a mortal wound from which he would die the next day. Union casualties were 625, while the Confederates were 175 dead and 300 prisoners. The loss of Stuart was a blow to the Confederacy.

Sheridan took his men south with orders to defeat his Confederate counterpart, J. E. B. Stuart, disrupt Rebel supply lines, and threaten Richmond, Virginia.

MAY

12

1917

THE TENTH BATTLE OF THE ISONZO An Italian offensive began against Austro-Hungarian forces during World War I.

MAY

13

1940

GERMAN TROOPS CROSS THE MEUSE RIVER The troops of XIX Panzer Corps crossed the river at Sedan in France to create a "panzer corridor" to split Allied armies in two.

MAY 14 1509

FRENCH VICTORY LEADS TO VENICE LOSSES Venice lost many of its mainland possessions after the Venetians were defeated at Agnadello in northern Italy.

MAY 15 1864

CADETS JOIN THE BATTLE OF NEW MARKET The participation of the Virginia Military Institute cadets led General Breckinridge to defeat Union General Sigel.

MAY 16 1811

BLOODY BATTLE 6,000 Allied soldiers and 7,000 Frenchmen lost their lives in four hours of combat in La Albuera, a village in Extremadura, Spain, during the Peninsular War.

MAY 17 1940

DE GAULLE'S 4TH ARMORED DIVISION IS BADLY MAULED In the Battle of France, General de Gaulle's division was badly mauled near Laon and forced to withdraw.

MAY 18 1794

FRENCH VICTORY The 70,000-strong French Revolutionary Army defeated an army of 74,000 composed of Austrian, British, and Hanoverian troops at Tourcoing, France.

MAY

1643

THE END OF SPANISH MILITARY POWER

The Battle of Rocroi in northern France, during the Thirty Years' War, foretold the eclipse of Spain and the emergence of France. Rocroi was also notable for the emergence of the French general Louis de Bourbon, Duc d'Enghien, whose army of 23,000 men confronted the Spanish general Francisco de Melo's 27,000 troops. The Spanish had been besieging Rocroi, west of the Meuse River.

Both armies deployed with their infantry in the center and cavalry on the wings. D'Enghien attacked with both wings of his army, the cavalry on the right proving successful while those on the left were worsted by the Spanish horsemen. The decisive moment came when d'Enghien led French cavalry through the enemy center, separating the Spanish front-line *tercios* from the less experienced Italian, German, and Walloon infantry, behind them, which fled, and going on to attack the Spanish cavalry on the left in the rear. The Spanish horsemen fled.

This forced the Spanish tercios to retreat. D'Enghien launched several attacks against them before they were decimated in a last stand. For the loss of 4,000 men, he had inflicted losses of 21,000 on the Spanish.

▶ The Spanish defeat the French at the Battle of Rocroi, during the Thirty Years' War.

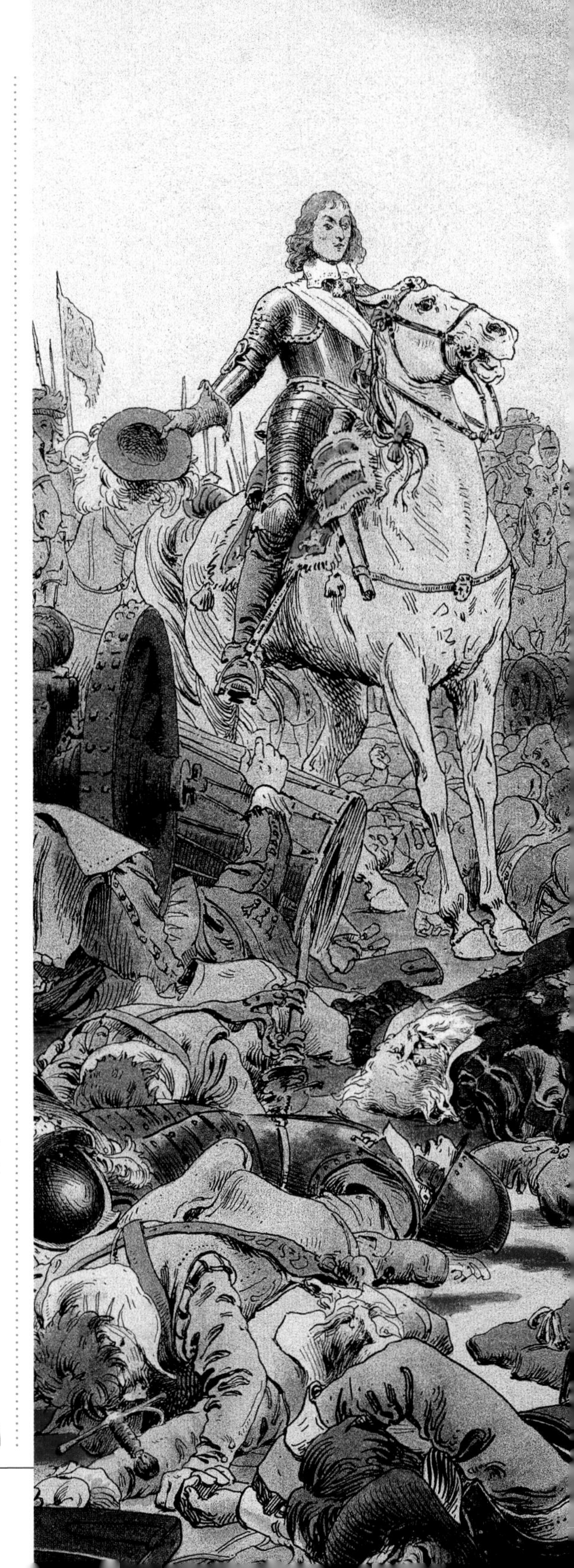

MAY

1217

CLASH AT LINCOLN DURING THE BARONS' WAR

The Battle of Lincoln was a turning point in the Barons' War and led to Louis returning to France for good.

The First Barons' War was a civil war between England's barons and King John, brought about by John's bad faith after signing the Magna Carta on June 15, 1215. The conflict also involved Scottish and French invasions in support of the rebels.

As a result of King John's reneging on the terms of Magna Carta, England descended into civil war between royalist forces and rebel barons who invited Prince Louis of France to take the English throne.

In May 1217, Lincoln Castle was besieged by the French, leading William Marshal, First Earl of Pembroke, to raise a royalist army and march to its relief. Pembroke and his knights, sergeants, and crossbowmen entered the city on the 20th, routing the French in front of the castle. The Battle of Lincoln was a turning point in the Barons' War and led to Louis returning to France for good.

MAY

1809

NAPOLEON CHECKED ON THE DANUBE

On this day the French emperor was mauled by the Austrians at the Battle of Aspern–Essling, near Vienna, Austria. After crossing the Danube via a single bridge onto the Isle of Lobau in his search for the Austrian Army, Napoleon was attacked by the Archduke Charles with more than 100,000 troops.

The next day, May 22, the French position worsened when they began to run out of ammunition, and although 73,000 Frenchmen were now in action, Napoleon ordered a retreat, with 22,000 casualties for no results. The emperor had had a lucky escape.

ALSO ON THIS DAY

1864

The Battle of Spotsylvania, an inconclusive engagement in which Union troops tried to break Confederate field defenses in Virginia during the American Civil War, ends.

BLOOD IN THE STREETS OF ST. ALBANS

During England's Wars of the Roses, the Lancastrian King Henry VI was defending the Hertfordshire town of St. Albans, which had a ditch and strong gates. The Yorkist rebels led by Richard, Duke of York, attacked the town in what became the First Battle of St. Albans.

The defenders had around 2,000 men, the Yorkists 3,000, their attacks at first being held up by barricades. But then the Earl of Warwick, the Kingmaker, ordered his 500 longbowmen to shoot at the barricades, which caused the royalist defenders to abandon them. This allowed the Yorkists to flood into the town, capturing King Henry himself.

ALSO ON THIS DAY

334BC

Alexander the Great defeats a Persian army, which includes Greek mercenaries, at the Battle of Granicus, the first of three major battles fought between Alexander and the Persian Empire.

FRENCH DEFEAT IN THE SPANISH NETHERLANDS

Louis XIV's insatiable desire to expand France's borders and prestige led to the War of the Spanish Succession (1702–13). In 1706, he ordered Marshal Villeroi to take his 60,000 troops east from the Dyle River to the Meuse. On the way, he was intercepted by the Duke of Marlborough with 50,000 men of an Anglo-Dutch-German army, at the village of Ramillies.

In the Battle of Ramillies, Marlborough feigned an attack on the French left, causing Villeroi to reinforce it with troops from his center and right. Marlborough's 25,000 cavalry then struck the opposite French flank and rolled up the entire French line, killing, wounding, or capturing 15,000 of the enemy. The victory allowed Marlborough to drive the French from almost the whole of the Spanish Netherlands.

Louis XIV's insatiable desire to expand France's borders and prestige led to the War of the Spanish Succession (1702–13).

MAY

1941

FIFTEEN MINUTES OF SLAUGHTER IN THE ATLANTIC

The Battle of Denmark Strait (between Greenland and Iceland) during World War II was a brief naval clash that lasted 15 minutes. It was fought between the German battleship *Bismarck* and cruiser *Prinz Eugen*, and the British battleships *Hood* and *King George V* and cruisers *Suffolk* and *Norfolk*.

The battle began with the British battleships opening fire on the German vessels, without effect. But when the *Bismarck* returned fire with her 15-inch guns, *Hood* was hit twice and exploded, sinking with the loss 1,397 officers and crew (the Royal Navy's largest loss of life from a single vessel). *King George V* was hit by seven shells, forcing her to break off the battle, but not before hitting *Bismarck* with three shells that caused her to list and drastically reduced her range, speed, and seakeeping ability. As a result, *Bismarck* was forced to turn southeast, toward France.

The Royal Navy, already keen to prevent *Bismarck* from ranging at will in the Atlantic, had even more reason to sink the battleship after the loss of *Hood*. It would have its revenge three days later when ships of the British Home Fleet sank *Bismarck*. The loss made Hitler very cautious about future German surface-ship operations against Britain's critical Atlantic sea lanes.

▲ The battleship *Bismarck* fires continuously during the Battle of Denmark Strait.

THE BLOODIEST BATTLE FOUGHT IN THE SHENANDOAH VALLEY

During the American Civil War, Virginia's Shenandoah Valley was the breadbasket of the Confederacy. It was therefore a target for the Union, which sent troops into the valley. In May 1862, one such body under General Banks was at Winchester where it turned to face the 17,000 soldiers of General "Stonewall" Jackson. Banks' 10,000 men occupied a fairly strong position south of the town. However, at the Battle of Winchester, fought on May 25, the Confederates broke through the Union line, forcing Banks and his men to flee back toward the Potomac River. Banks lost 62 soldiers and saw 243 wounded and 1,700 captured or missing. Confederate losses were 68 killed and 329 wounded.

Virginia's Shenandoah Valley was the breadbasket of the Confederacy. It was therefore a target for the Union.

A SIDESHOW IN THE THIRTY YEARS' WAR

In 1640, Portugal threw off the Spanish yoke. But the Spanish directed several plots against King John IV of Portugal. This provoked John to launch an invasion of western Spain, General de Albuquerque leading 6,000 infantry, 1,100 cavalry, and six cannon toward Badajoz. Opposing them were 4,000 infantry and 1,700 cavalry under the Baron of Mollingen. The two forces met near the town of Montijo.

The Battle of Montijo was an amateur affair, the Spanish first routing the Portuguese cavalry and capturing the cannon. The rest of the Spanish Army then began looting, which allowed the Portuguese to re-form and recapture the guns. Both sides claimed victory, each with around 3,000 dead and wounded.

ALSO ON THIS DAY

1573

At the Battle of Haarlemmermeer, a Spanish fleet of 100 defeated a Dutch force of 150 warships attempting to lift the siege of Haarlem, during the Dutch War of Independence.

MAY

27

1905

HUMILIATION FOR THE RUSSIAN NAVY

Following an unbroken series of Japanese successes in the Russo-Japanese War, Tsar Nicholas II ordered Russia's Baltic Fleet to the Far East. Commanded by Admiral Zinovi Rozhdestvenski, the fleet comprised 45 ships, including seven battleships and six cruisers.

On this day, the Russian fleet sailed into the Tsushima Strait leading to the Sea of Japan. Here it was intercepted by Admiral Heihachiro Togo's Japanese fleet, which was of a comparable size to the Russian force. But qualitatively, the Japanese ships and their crews were far superior. Togo attacked at a speed of 16 knots, his ships struck the slower-moving Russian vanguard at an angle, and in 30 minutes the quicker-firing Japanese guns had sunk one Russian battleship, crippled another, and scattered the Russian fleet. By nightfall, three more Russian battleships had been sunk.

Under cover of darkness, the shaken Rozhdestvenski led the remains of his fleet toward the Russian port of Vladivostok. But his agony was not yet over, for Togo sent his destroyers and torpedo boats to pursue the enemy. Three more Russian vessels were sunk that night, and the next day the pursuit continued. By the end of the Battle of Tsushima, all but 12 vessels of the Russian fleet had been sunk, captured, or driven ashore in the greatest sea battle since Trafalgar.

▼ The Japanese battleship *Shikishima* participated in the Battle of Tsushima.

MAY

1982

PARA ATTACK AT GOOSE GREEN

Britain's Parachute Regiment is an elite force, designed to fight and defeat a better-armed and numerically superior enemy in any part of the world. In the 1982 Falklands War between Britain and Argentina, the Paras were deployed to great effect.

On May 28, the men of the 2nd Parachute Battalion (2 Para) were engaged in an assault against Argentine forces around the settlement of Goose Green, East Falkland. The terrain around Goose Green is rolling and covered with thick gorse, which can impede movement. The ground is also sodden, which makes movement slow and exhausting.

The attack began at 06:35, the Paras coming under anti-tank and grenade attack but charging forward to storm Argentine trenches near Burntside House. But the Paras, once under artillery fire, became pinned down around the positions of Boca House and Darwin Hill. It was at this point that Colonel "H" Jones fell while leading an attack. (Jones would be awarded a posthumous Victoria Cross for his bravery.) His death energized the Paras, who charged forward with fixed bayonets to break through Argentine lines and capture Darwin Hill.

The Paras then advanced on the settlement of Goose Green itself and dug in around Argentine positions. The Argentinians in Goose Green were now surrounded, without any hope of relief. They surrendered the next day. The Paras had lost 15 soldiers and 30 were wounded but they had captured 1,300 prisoners.

▼ Pilots and crew prepare a U.S. fighter aircraft prior to an airlift, in Goose Green, East Falkland.

MAY

1453

THE END OF THE BYZANTINE EMPIRE

For 1,200 years the walls of Constantinople (now Istanbul) had resisted all enemies, but in April 1453, Ottoman naval and land forces under Sultan Mehmet II, "the Conqueror," ringed the city. Mehmet commanded 100,000 men against 7,000 defenders.

Mehmet sealed off the city by land and sea and began bombarding Constantinople with his huge cannon. He also transported ships overland on rollers into the Golden Horn (the city's main harbor), which signaled the death knell for the defenders. Ottoman forces swarmed into the city on May 29, capturing the former capital of the Eastern Roman Empire.

ALSO ON THIS DAY

1176

The Lombard League, a medieval alliance sponsored by the Pope to counter the ambitions of the Holy Roman Emperor, defeats the forces of Emperor Frederick Barbarossa at the Battle of Legnano.

MAY

1434

THE END OF THE HUSSITE CIVIL WAR

The Hussites (followers of the Czech religious reformer Jan Hus) defeated several crusades against them in the early 15th century, but during the same period they often fought among themselves.

On May 30, at Lipany in Slovakia, 25 miles (40 km) east of Prague, 14,000 Bohemian League soldiers confronted an army of Hussite radicals 10,700-strong. The radicals constructed a wagon-fort on a hill, both armies observing each other for some time before the League attempted to negotiate. Mistaking this for weakness, the radicals left their strong position and attacked down the hill. The League soldiers began shooting from the cover of their own wagon-forts. At the same time, the League cavalry infiltrated the radicals' wagon-fort. The result was the collapse and destruction of the Hussites' army. The Battle of Lipany ended the Hussite Civil War.

When the League tried to negotiate, the radicals mistook this for weakness and left their strong position, attacking down the hill.

JUTLAND: LARGEST SURFACE BATTLE IN NAVAL HISTORY

The Imperial German Navy's High Seas Fleet (Admiral Reinhard Scheer) had been deployed to Denmark's Jutland Peninsula to attack Allied shipping and ease the naval blockade on Germany; the British Grand Fleet (Admiral Sir John Jellicoe) sailed to engage it. The scene was thus set for the Battle of Jutland, a huge naval engagement involving 151 British ships and 99 German vessels.

When the battle began, the Germans had the advantage of greater visibility due to the position of the sun. At just after 14:00 hours, the battlecruiser *Indefatigable* was hit and exploded, 1,000 crew being killed. Twenty minutes later, the cruiser *Queen Mary* was sunk. The *Invincible* was sunk at 18:30 hours.

The battle raged into the night, ships crashing into each other and many being badly damaged. Jellicoe hoped to continue the action the next day, but Scheer broke off the battle during the night and headed for home.

In the Battle of Jutland the British came off worse, losing 14 ships and more than 6,000 men compared to nine German ships lost and more than 2,500 casualties. However, the Royal Navy was able to continue its crippling blockade of Germany.

▼ The Royal Navy Invincible-class battlecruiser H.M.S. *Invincible* of the 2nd Battlecruiser Squadron was sunk during the Battle of Jutland.

June

JUNE 1

1794

THE "GLORIOUS FIRST OF JUNE"

It was the first naval battle between Britain and France during the French Revolutionary Wars. Four hundred miles (640 km) off France's Atlantic seaboard, a British fleet of 34 warships under the command of Admiral Earl Howe engaged Rear Admiral Villaret-Joyeuse's 26 warships, which were sailing to escort a grain convoy from America. France was gripped by a food crisis, so the food being transported by the convoy was critical to the survival of the revolutionary regime.

In a hard-fought battle characterized by a series of single combats between ships, 7,000 Frenchmen and 1,000 British were killed or wounded, 11 British and 12 French ships were dismasted, six French ships were captured, and another sunk. The grain convoy reached France unimpeded.

▼ Admiral Lord Howe on the quarterdeck of his flagship, H.M.S. *Queen Charlotte*, as the Royal Navy British Channel fleet engages the French Atlantic fleet.

JUNE

1653

ENGLISH NAVAL VICTORY AT GABBARD BANK

The two-day battle of Gabbard Bank (off the coast of Suffolk, England) began on June 2. An action during the Anglo-Dutch War of 1652–4, it was the first battle in which the new English fighting instructions were put into effect: ships were to sail in line formation and crews should board enemy ships only after they had been crippled by gunfire.

The two fleets had around 100 vessels each but the Dutch ships were low on ammunition and had suffered heavy damage, and the crew were thoroughly demoralized by the superior firepower of the English ships. The next day the English captured eleven vessels and sank a further six. The English now controlled the English Channel and the North Sea.

After the battle, the English general-at-sea George Monck imposed a blockade on Dutch ports, which had a devastating effect on the economy of the Netherlands.

It was the first battle in which the new English fighting instructions were put into effect.

JUNE

1864

A BLOODY DAY AT COLD HARBOR

In June 1864, during the American Civil War, the road junction at Cold Harbor, 10 miles (16 km) north of the Confederate capital of Richmond, Virginia, hosted a series of costly engagements, which revealed the folly of launching troops against well-defended entrenchments.

The Confederate commander, General Robert E. Lee, had continually frustrated the offensives of the Union commander-in-chief, General Ulysses S. Grant, but on June 3 Grant believed his great superiority in numbers would finally be able to break the Confederate line. He assembled three of his corps—VII, III, and XVII, a total of 108,000 men—to attack the Confederates at Cold Harbor (though neither Grant nor his second-in-command, George Meade, had observed the Confederate line, which was heavily fortified). Defending the earthworks were 59,000 Confederates of I and III Corps. The Union soldiers attacked but were immediately stopped by murderous frontal and enfilade fire, which killed or wounded 7,000 Federal troops in 60 minutes. Confederate losses were around 1,500.

Both armies held their positions until June 12, shooting at each other across no-man's land. Despite his victory, Lee could not prevent Grant from laying siege to Petersburg at the end of June.

TURNING POINT AT MIDWAY

In mid-1942, the Japanese Navy was determined to sink the U.S. Navy's aircraft carriers and extend Japan's defensive perimeter in the Pacific. To this end, the navy's commander-in-chief, Admiral Isoroku Yamamoto, ordered the capture of Midway Island in the Hawaiian archipelago. However, forewarned of the Japanese plan by codebreakers, Admiral Chester Nimitz, Commander-in-Chief, Pacific Ocean Areas, assembled a naval force that included three aircraft carriers to intercept the Japanese ships.

On June 4, the two forces clashed off Midway Island. Japanese aircraft that had been attacking U.S. positions on the island were caught on deck by U.S. carrier aircraft while they were being refueled and rearmed. The carriers *Akagi* and *Kaga* were soon ablaze, the latter sinking in the evening with the loss of 800 men. *Soryu* was struck by two bombs and within 20 minutes was aflame and had to be abandoned. The fourth Japanese carrier, *Hiryu*, managed to launch its aircraft, which attacked and crippled the U.S. carrier *Yorktown*. However, U.S. carrier aircraft then struck the *Hiryu*, reducing it to a flaming wreck.

The Battle of Midway was one of the most decisive battles in history. In a single day Japan had lost half its carrier fleet, plus 322 naval aircraft. It never recovered from the loss.

▼ Pilots and crew prepare the fighter planes prior to their take-off for the Battle of Midway.

SIX DAYS THAT CHANGED THE WORLD

The Six-Day War of 1967 changed the geopolitical map of the Middle East and established a legacy that is still felt today.

On June 5, Israel's defense forces unleashed a surprise attack on their belligerent Arab neighbors, knocking out the Egyptian, Syrian, and Jordanian air forces in a matter of hours. In the five days that followed, the Israeli Army routed the armies of Egypt, Jordan, and Syria, capturing the Gaza Strip and Sinai desert from Egypt, the Golan Heights from Syria, and the West Bank and East Jerusalem from Jordan. It was one of the most complete and stunning military victories in modern warfare, and would lead to animosity between Jews and Arabs that endures to this day.

ALSO ON THIS DAY

1288

Duke John of Brabant defeats Archbishop Siegfried of Cologne at the Battle of Worringen, Germany, fought for possession of the Duchy of Limburg. The duke loses 40 men, the archbishop 1,100.

DAY OF DAYS IN NORMANDY

The Allied invasion of Normandy in World War II, codenamed Operation Overlord, began on this day. In order to land 50,000 soldiers in the initial assault on five beaches—Utah, Omaha, Gold, Juno, and Sword—the Allies had amassed 138 major warships, 221 smaller vessels, 4,000 landing craft, 805 merchant ships, 59 blockships, and 300 small craft. Overhead, 11,000 aircraft ensured Allied air superiority.

U.S. and British paratroopers were dropped behind the beaches on the night of June 5/6, and the landings themselves were supported by a massive naval bombardment and 14,600 air sorties. By the end of the day, despite stiff German resistance on Omaha, all five beaches were secure. For the loss of 2,500 men, the Allies had opened a second front in Europe.

By the end of the day, despite stiff German resistance on Omaha, all five beaches were secure.

JUNE

1917

THE BIGGEST BANG OF WORLD WAR I

To capture the Wytschaete–Messines ridge on the Western Front, which allowed the Germans to observe Allied movements in the Ypres salient, tunnels were dug beneath the German positions. The Battle of Messines, which began on June 7, opened with explosives being detonated in 19 mines under German positions.

Tunnels were dug beneath the German positions in order to capture the Wytschaete–Messines ridge on the Western Front.

British and Empire troops, protected by a creeping artillery barrage, then attacked the shocked Germans. The New Zealand Division captured the village of Messines, the 16th (Irish) Division and 36th (Ulster) Division seizing the village of Wytschaete in one of the most successful operations of the war on the Western Front. All subsequent German attempts to retake the ridge were unsuccessful.

JUNE

1982

CAPTURE OF THE TOWN OF JEZZINE The first battle between Israeli and Syrian forces in the Bekaa Valley during the Lebanon War ended in an Israeli victory.

JUNE

1862

CONFEDERATE JACKSON DEFEATS FEDERAL TROOPS Jackson gained control of the upper and middle Shenandoah Valley after victory at Port Republic, Virginia.

JUNE

1619

PROTESTANT MERCENARY ARMY IS DEFEATED The army was defeated early in the Thirty Years' War, at Sablat, Bohemia, by a Catholic Imperial army.

JUNE

1864

CAPTURE AND RETREAT Union cavalry under General Sheridan captured Trevilian Station, Virginia, during the American Civil War but were forced to retreat the next day.

JUNE

910

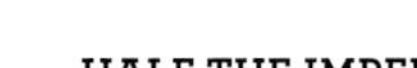

HALF THE IMPERIAL ARMY IS KILLED IN BATTLE Magyar (Hungarian) troops defeated the Frankish Imperial forces of Louis the Child at Lechfeld near Augsburg, Bavaria.

JUNE

1982

BRITAIN'S 2 PARA CAPTURES WIRELESS RIDGE It was one of the last actions during the Falklands War; the Argentinians surrendered the next day.

JUNE

1800

NAPOLEON BONAPARTE TRIUMPHANT IN MARENGO The Austrians were defeated in Marengo, Piedmont, Italy, resulting in the French occupation of Lombardy.

1918

AUSTRIAN DISASTER ON THE PIAVE RIVER

During World War I, following the Italian defeat at Caporetto in 1917, the Austrians were determined to deliver a knockout blow against the Italians. To this end, they assembled their 5th, 6th, 10th, and 11th armies—58 divisions—which launched the Battle of Piave on June 15.

The 10th and 11th armies made no progress, while the 5th and 6th managed to advance 3 miles (4.6 km) across the Piave. But the Italians fought back fiercely and by the time the battle ended on June 23, the Austrians had suffered a total of 150,000 casualties for no result.

ALSO ON THIS DAY

1219

Danish Crusaders led by their king, Valdemar II, defeat pagan Estonians at the Battle of Lyndanisse (modern-day Tallinn), thus establishing a new Danish colony in the Baltic.

1487

LAST BATTLE OF THE WARS OF THE ROSES

King Henry VII defeated an army of Yorkist rebels at the Battle of Stoke Field. Henry's army of 15,000 clashed with the 8,000 men of the pretender Lambert Simnel outside Newark, Nottinghamshire, Henry's vanguard at first being driven back. The Yorkist army contained 2,000 mercenary German and Swiss pikemen, who maintained a tight formation, but were showered with arrows by archers commanded by Henry's best lieutenant, the Earl of Oxford. The phalanx of pikemen was shot to pieces, prompting the rest of the Yorkist army to flee in panic. In the subsequent pursuit, up to half the Yorkists were cut down.

ALSO ON THIS DAY

1815

During the Waterloo campaign, Marshal Ney engages the Duke of Wellington at the strategic crossroads of Quatre Bras, thus preventing the British from reinforcing the Prussian Army at Ligny.

FIRST PITCHED BATTLE OF THE AMERICAN REVOLUTIONARY WAR

Following the fights at Lexington and Concord, British troops under General Sir Thomas Gage concentrated in the city of Boston, Massachusetts. This drew in rebel militia, who conducted a siege under the leadership of General Artemas Ward. Some 1,600 colonists under Colonel William Prescott began fortifying Breed's Hill (they had been instructed to fortify Bunker Hill, which was further forward) on the Charlestown Peninsula. In response, Gage ordered a frontal assault on the position. On June 17, General Sir William Howe, with 2,100 Redcoats, made a frontal assault on Breed's Hill.

The Redcoats were struck by cannon and musket fire that twice drove them back. Reinforced by 400 fresh troops under General Sir Henry Clinton, Howe launched a third attack that drove the Americans, who were running short of powder, off the hill. The nearby Bunker Hill was also abandoned by the colonists.

The Battle of Bunker Hill, so called because the Americans thought they were on the hill of that name, cost the British 1,150 killed or wounded—nearly half of the force engaged—while American losses were 450 killed and wounded.

The Battle of Bunker Hill was so called because the Americans thought they were on the hill of that name.

An illustration after a painting by John Trumbull shows British military forces reaching the top of Breed's Hill, where they clash with colonial militia during the Battle of Bunker Hill.

THE FINAL DRAMA OF THE NAPOLEONIC WARS

After his return from exile on Elba in March 1815, Napoleon, in response to the Allies forming a Seventh Coalition against him, planned first to defeat the Prussian marshal Blücher before going to battle with the Duke of Wellington's British Army. The result of his bold plan was that he found himself facing Wellington near the Belgian village of Waterloo on June 18.

Napoleon with 72,000 troops faced Wellington, with 68,000 men deployed on the ridge of Mont Saint-Jean, across a rain-soaked battlefield. The French emperor was determined to fight a battle of attrition against Wellington, the action beginning at 11:30 hours with the French failing to capture the strongpoint of Hougoumont on Wellington's right flank. The mass French infantry attack launched at 13:30 hours failed to break the British center, as did Marshal Ney's massed cavalry charges later in the afternoon. But the French did eventually take the strongpoint of La Haye Sainte, threatening Wellington's center. The French Imperial Guard then attacked, expecting to win the battle, but were repulsed. French morale began to break, compounded by the arrival of the Prussians on their right flank.

The Battle of Waterloo cost the French 33,000 killed or taken prisoner, the British and Prussians 22,000. It also marked the end of an era of warfare.

▼ Wellington, center, is flanked on his left by Lord Uxbridge, his second-in-command, at Waterloo.

1306

A CLOSE CALL FOR ROBERT THE BRUCE

Robert the Bruce had been crowned King Robert I of Scotland in March 1306, having murdered one of his rivals, John Comyn, beforehand. Unfortunately for Robert, Comyn had been a friend of the Earl of Pembroke, whom the English King Edward I sent north with an army to bring Robert to heel.

King Robert fled to the Scottish Highlands, though his wife was captured and became a prisoner of the English for eight years.

Pembroke with around 2,200 men clashed with Robert's 2,500 troops near the village of Methven, west of Perth, in a bitterly fought contest. The English prevailed and King Robert fled to the Scottish Highlands, though his wife was captured and became a prisoner of the English for eight years. It was while Bruce was hiding in the caves and islands of western Scotland that he was allegedly inspired by the perseverance of a spider. His fight back began in May 1307 when he won a minor victory at the Battle of Loudoun Hill.

451

ATTILA, SCOURGE OF GOD

The Battle of the Catalaunian Plains, also known as the Battle of Châlons, is considered one of the most decisive battles in history because it stopped the Huns destroying what remained of Classical civilization in the West.

A Roman army and allies commanded by Flavius Aetius fought a Hun army led by Attila. Ironically, Aetius, the Roman commander in the West, had previously relied on Huns to staff his armies, but now had to recruit Alans, Visigoths, Franks, Britons, and Saxons to fight them. The battle lasted all day, each side launching charges and countercharges. By evening, Attila had suffered heavy losses and withdrew to his camp, the Huns retreating back across the Rhine the next day.

The battle is considered one of the most decisive battles in history because it stopped the Huns destroying what remained of Classical civilization in the West.

CRUSHING THE REBELLION OF THE UNITED IRISHMEN

The Irish Rebellion of 1798 aimed to throw the British out of Ireland. However, poor coordination, infiltration by spies, and lack of weapons meant that the rebellion was contained fairly easily by the British Army. The final battle of the uprising took place at Vinegar Hill in the County of Wexford.

The Irishmen, commanded by Father John Murphy, numbered around 20,000 but had few muskets, being armed mostly with pikes, and no artillery. The British troops, on the other hand, were all armed with muskets and supported by artillery. The plan of the British commander, General Gerard Lake, was to surround the hill and capture the only rebel escape route: the bridge of the Slaney River to the west.

Dividing his army into four columns, Lake ordered an attack following an artillery bombardment, which caused hundreds of Irish deaths. A detachment of British troops was sent to capture the nearby town of Enniscorthy, but was repulsed with loss. A second attack forced the rebels out of the town, but they held Slaney Bridge to secure the withdrawal of the decimated rebels on Vinegar Hill, now under infantry, cavalry, and artillery attack. Irish losses were 1,200, those of the British 100. Father Murphy was later captured and hanged.

▼ Members of the republican United Irishmen fighting British troops at the Battle of Vinegar Hill in Co. Wexford, Ireland.

JUNE 22 1941

BARBAROSSA: THUNDER IN THE EAST

The German Wehrmacht began the greatest land battle in history when it launched the invasion of the Soviet Union in 1941, during World War II. Under the code name Barbarossa, three million German and Axis troops organized in three army groups, supported by over 3,000 tanks and 2,200 aircraft, pulverized the defending Red Army units. Hundreds of thousands of Red Army troops were either killed or captured as panzer columns struck deep into Russian territory.

The Red Army began Barbarossa with 5.5 million troops; by the end of October this number had been reduced to 2.2 million. But the Russians were still fighting, the Germans had failed to take Moscow and Leningrad, and the Russian winter was approaching. Barbarossa had failed.

The Germans had failed to take Moscow and Leningrad, and the Russian winter was approaching. Barbarossa had failed.

JUNE 23 1757

CLIVE OF INDIA'S MASTERPIECE

The Battle of Plassey, fought on this day in Bengal, India, was an example of the superiority of well-trained and well-armed professional soldiers over ill-trained and poorly armed civilians pressed into military service.

Major General Robert Clive, with 850 British troops, 12 cannon, and 1,200 sepoys (Indian infantry), met the Nawab of Bengal's army of 52,000 men and 53 cannon at Plassey. Clive's army was deployed in a mango grove, and proceeded to engage in an artillery duel with the enemy for four hours. A downpour put all the Nawab's cannon out of action, and his cavalry was repulsed by grapeshot. Clive then ordered his men to advance, which caused a rout in the enemy army. For the loss of 65 casualties, Robert Clive had won the vast province of Bengal for the British East India Company.

The Battle of Plassey in Bengal, India, was an example of the superiority of professional troops over ill-trained levies.

JUNE 24

1314

VICTORY FOR THE SCOTS AT BANNOCKBURN

King Edward II of England lacked the character and the military skill of his father—inadequacies that would be taken advantage of by Robert the Bruce, King of Scotland.

In 1314, Edward attempted to relieve Stirling Castle with 2,000 knights and 15,000 foot soldiers. Robert had only 500 light cavalry and 7,000 foot soldiers, but was a much better commander. He assumed a defensive position behind a stream and dug pits to hamper the English cavalry, thereby repulsing Edward's attack. The English king then attempted a night march to outflank the Scots, which left his knights stranded in boggy ground. Bruce then charged the strung-out English foot and routed them. The English knights, unable to maneuver, soon broke, leaving 500 dead behind; 11,000 English infantry were also killed.

The Battle of Bannockburn led to the independence of Scotland.

King Edward II of England lacked the character and the military skill of his father.

JUNE 25

1876

CUSTER'S LAST STAND

"There are not enough Indians in the world to defeat the seventh cavalry."

—GEORGE ARMSTRONG CUSTER

The Battle of the Little Bighorn, fought on this day near the Little Bighorn River in Montana Territory, was the worst defeat for the U.S. Army in the Plains Indian War.

In response to broken treaty agreements, Sioux and Cheyenne warriors joined up with Lakota leaders Sitting Bull and Crazy Horse in Montana. By late spring 1876, they had 10,000 warriors under their command. The U.S. Army sent three columns of troops to disperse the warriors, one of which comprised 600 men of the 7th Cavalry under the command of George Armstrong Custer. Without waiting for reinforcements, Custer rode into the Valley of the Little Bighorn. When his men were spotted by a few warriors, Custer assumed they would warn Sitting Bull of his presence and scatter. He therefore decided to split his command into three groups to encircle Sitting Bull's camp. However, Custer's column of 210 men was itself attacked by up to 2,000 warriors and annihilated within an hour.

▶ *Custer's Last Stand* from the Battle of the Little Bighorn.

VICTORY FOR FRANCE AT FLEURUS

The Battle of Fleurus was a turning point in the War of the First Coalition against France. An advance by the French general Jean-Baptiste Jourdan into the Austrian Netherlands at the head of 70,000 troops was halted by a chiefly Austrian army of 50,000 soldiers, commanded by the Prince of Saxe-Coburg, at Fleurus in present-day Belgium.

The Austrian general deployed his army into five columns and sent them against the French. Though the Austrians pushed back both French wings, in the center Jourdan's men held and then counterattacked, throwing the Austrians back. The whole Austrian assault then petered out. But it had been a protracted and costly battle in which each side lost an estimated 5,000 men. Fleurus was also the first time in history that an aircraft decided the outcome of a battle (a French reconnaissance balloon kept Jourdan abreast of Austrian movements throughout the engagement).

Saxe-Coburg fell back across the Meuse River after the battle, allowing the French to annex the Austrian Netherlands. Holland capitulated in 1795, and Prussia and Spain dropped out of the war against France in the same year.

Fleurus had been a major strategic victory for revolutionary France.

The Battle of Fleurus was a turning point in the War of the First Coalition against France.

◀ Jean-Baptiste Jourdan's victory at the Battle of Fleurus.

1743

THE LAST TIME A BRITISH KING LED HIS TROOPS INTO BATTLE

During the War of the Austrian Succession, an English–Hanoverian–Hessian army, under the command of British King George II, was cornered by a French army led by Marshal Duc Adrien de Noailles in a defile between Aschaffenburg and Hanau, at the village of Dettingen on the Main River, Germany.

Noailles deployed a blocking force of 23,000 men to prevent the British from escaping west, and sent 12,000 to hit George's army from the east. But the blocking force attacked, to be counterattacked by the British with George himself leading his troops. The French line collapsed with 5,000 killed, and the route west was open. After their defeat at Dettingen, the French withdrew all their troops west of the Rhine River.

Noailles deployed a blocking force to prevent the British from escaping west, and sent 12,000 to hit George's army from the east.

1575

JAPANESE WARFARE IS CHANGED FOREVER

The warlord of the Tokugawa clan, Nobunaga Oda, led 38,000 troops to relieve the besieged Nagashino Castle in central Japan. The besiegers were Katsuyori Takeda's 15,000 troops, one-third of which were elite Samurai cavalry.

Receiving news of the approach of Oda's army, Takeda decided to meet him in open battle. Oda constructed a wooden palisade behind a stream where he placed 3,000 matchlock gunners under the command of Samurai officers, in a radical departure from traditional tactics.

Oda's gunners decimated Takeda's cavalry with their volleys and then the infantry that followed. In an eight-hour battle, Takeda lost 10,000 men before quitting the field. Oda lost fewer than 6,000 men.

ALSO ON THIS DAY

1778

George Washington's Continental Army and General Sir Henry Clinton's British Army fought an inconclusive battle at Monmouth Courthouse during the American Revolutionary War.

AUSTRIANS MAULED AT PARMA

Dynastic struggle could spread like a plague to engulf all Europe. So it was that the War of Polish Succession (1733–5) involved fighting in Poland, the Rhineland, and Italy. And it was in the latter theater that the Battle of Parma was fought, where Russia's ally Austria was pitted against France, Spain, and Savoy (Sardinia).

Unfortunately for Austrian emperor Charles VI, his troops in Italy were suffering from low morale and weak leadership. Thus, when they faced 60,000 French and Sardinian troops at Parma, 75 miles (120 km) southeast of Milan in present-day Italy, the 50,000 Austrians at first performed well enough, attacking and making headway in the face of Allied musket and artillery fire. But when their commander, Marshal Mercy, was killed by a musket ball, the Austrians faltered.

The Austrian second-in-command, Frederick of Württemberg, managed to re-establish order and the Austrian advance continued, reaching the walls of Parma itself. But they had lost over 6,000 killed and wounded, and stiffening Allied resistance was enough to compel them to withdraw. Though the Allies occupied the battlefield, their victory was a costly one: 4,000 French killed and wounded and 400 Sardinian casualties.

> **Unfortunately for Austrian Emperor Charles VI, his troops in Italy were suffering from low morale and weak leadership.**

ALSO ON THIS DAY

1644

A Royalist army led by King Charles I defeats a Parliamentary army under the command of Sir William Waller at the Battle of Cropredy Bridge, during the English Civil War.

1149

During the Second Crusade, a Seljuk force led by Nur ab-Din defeats an army led by Prince Raymond of Antioch at the Battle of Inab.

JUNE 30

763

BYZANTINES *VS.* BULGARS AT ANCHIALUS

The Byzantine Empire was a powerful civilization that endured for over 1,000 years after its establishment by the Roman emperor Constantine. One of the reasons for its endurance was the skill of its armies against a host of enemies.

In June 763, Emperor Constantine V sent a Byzantine expeditionary force of 800 ships and 9,600 cavalry to Thrace to defend the fortress of Anchialus on the Black Sea coast from Telets, ruler of the Bulgarian Empire. Constantine marched up through Thrace to link up with his horsemen at Anchialus.

Telets and his Bulgar army attacked the emperor on the 30th in a battle that raged from dawn till dusk. The size of each army is unknown, but contemporary reports allude to heavy casualties and many Bulgar prisoners being taken.

Constantine took the prisoners back to Constantinople, where they were put to death. Telets managed to escape but was killed by his own countrymen two years later due to the severity of the defeat at Anchialus. The fact that Constantine did not follow up his victory with an invasion of Bulgar territory suggests that his army suffered heavy losses, especially among its cavalry arm. Constantine would rule for another 12 years, until his death in 775.

▲ Telets, ruler of the Bulgarian Empire, and his Bulgar army attacks Emperor Constantine V's cavalry in a contemporary illustration.

CHAPTER
7
July

JULY

1916

FIRST DAY OF THE SOMME

The Somme Offensive in 1916 was originally a joint operation by Britain and France, but due to French losses at Verdun, it became a mainly British effort, over a 15-mile (24-km) front focused on the town of Bapaume. Despite a week-long artillery bombardment, many of the German defenses remained intact when the offensive was launched on July 1. In these seven days, the British artillery fired more than 1.5 million shells, exceeding the total number of shells fired by the British Army in the first 12 months of the war. A further quarter of a million shells would be fired on the day of the attack.

The British soldiers ran into a hail of machine-gun and artillery fire, which cut down thousands. It is testimony to the tenacity of British troops that they managed to capture some of their objectives. The 18th and 30th Divisions took all their objectives around Montauban, the 7th Division captured Mametz, and the 36th (Ulster) Division took the Schwaben redoubt (but was forced to abandon it due to exposed flanks). The French also achieved some success south of the Somme River.

But the cost in blood had been exorbitant. On this day, the British Army suffered 57,470 casualties, including 19,240 killed. It was the deadliest day in British military history. When the Somme Offensive finally ended on November 18, 1916, it had cost the British Army 420,000 casualties. The Germans had suffered losses of 650,000 and the French 195,000, for very little gain.

▼ The 39th Siege Battery artillery in action in the Fricourt-Mametz Valley during the Battle of the Somme, France.

JULY

1644

CAVALIER DEFEAT AT MARSTON MOOR

After victories in the first two years of the English Civil War, King Charles' Royalists had gained control of much of England. But a treaty between Scotland and Parliament led to a Scottish army crossing into England, tipping the scales of war in favor of the Parliament. A combined Scottish-Parliamentarian army had soon besieged the city of York. Charles' nephew, Prince Rupert of the Rhine, went to relieve the city and forced the army to lift their siege. Rupert and the king's commander in the North, the Earl of Newcastle, then pursued the army and fought them on July 2, 6 miles (9.6 km) to the west of York, on Marston Moor.

Both armies deployed their cavalry on the wings and their infantry in the center. The battle began with Roundhead artillery opening fire at 19:00 hours, then both right wings charged and were defeated by the opposing wings. But the left-wing Roundhead cavalry under Oliver Cromwell rode around the back of the Cavaliers and attacked the triumphant horsemen, forcing them to flee. The isolated Royalist infantry then fled.

The Battle of Marston Moor cost the king 4,000 killed and 1,500 captured, and lost him the North.

▲ Oliver Cromwell is shown leading a charge after being wounded in his right arm during the Battle of Marston Moor.

CONFEDERATE HIGH TIDE AT GETTYSBURG

The three-day battle of Gettysburg had started well for Robert E. Lee's Army of Northern Virginia, Confederate troops taking Gettysburg on July 1. But the next day, Lee's hopes of victory were frustrated when Union forces could not be ejected from Little Round Top and Culp's Hill. The Union commander, General George Meade, was continually reinforced to bring his strength up to 88,000 men compared to Lee's 83,000. But Lee was determined to win and decided to mount a major assault on July 3 against Cemetery Ridge.

Meade had guessed Lee's intentions and had strengthened his center with troops and artillery. Shortly after 13:00 hours, 140 Confederate cannon opened fire on Cemetery Ridge, and an hour later, three divisions under Generals Pickett, Trimble, and Pettigrew—15,000 troops—left the wooded cover of Seminary Ridge to march three-quarters of a mile (1.2 km) across an open field and up the hill. As they did so, they were caught in a hail of small-arms and artillery fire that decimated their ranks. Only George Pickett and 150 men reached the crest of Cemetery Ridge, where they were soon routed.

Lee had lost the Battle of Gettysburg, sustaining 23,063 casualties to the Union's 23,049. But the South had effectively lost the Civil War.

THE HORNS OF HATTIN

The Battle of Hattin destroyed the military power of the Christian Kingdom of Jerusalem.

The hapless King Guy de Lusignan of Jerusalem marched his 1,200 knights and 15,000 foot soldiers into waterless terrain where they were surrounded by Sultan Saladin's 12,000 cavalry and 20,000 foot soldiers. Guy was attempting to relieve the besieged town of Tiberius on Lake Galilee, but Saladin's cavalry harassed the Christian army, which took up position on the site of an ancient hill fort on the twin peaks known as the Horns of Hattin. The resulting battle resulted in over 1,000 knights being killed and most of the Christian infantry being captured and enslaved. King Guy was among those captured.

ALSO ON THIS DAY

1863

Union forces defeat a Confederate attempt to relieve the pressure on the besieged city of Vicksburg at the Battle of Helena, Arkansas, during the American Civil War.

JULY

1943

THE GREATEST TANK BATTLE IN HISTORY

The Battle of Kursk was Nazi Germany's last great offensive on the Eastern Front in World War II. Code-named Operation Citadel, it aimed to destroy huge numbers of Red Army troops in the Kursk salient, 280 miles (450 km) southwest of Moscow. But the Red Army commander, Georgy Zhukov, had anticipated the German attack and had reinforced the salient with one million troops, 20,000 artillery pieces, 6,000 anti-tank guns, 5,000 tanks, and hundreds of rocket launchers.

When the German Ninth Army (335,000 men, 590 tanks, and 424 assault guns), and the 4th Panzer Army and Army Detachment Kempf (350,000 men, 1,269 tanks, and 245 assault guns) attacked on July 5, they ran straight into the Soviet defenses. The Battle of Kursk would rage until July 13, ending in a German defeat, the decimation of its Panzer arm, and ultimately the loss of the war on the Eastern Front. The turning point of the battle occurred on July 12 at the town of Prokhorovka—a massive tank battle stopping the German 4th Panzer Army in its tracks.

▼ Red Army infantry and SU-76 self-propelled guns assault German positions during the Battle Of Kursk.

CHARLES VIII OF FRANCE ESCAPES A TRAP AT FORNOVO

The ambitious Charles VIII of France was withdrawing from Italy when he was ambushed by Venetian forces in the north of the country, at Fornovo in the province of Parma.

The Swiss were able to drive off the Venetians, allowing the French army to escape.

Charles commanded 4,500 men-at-arms, 3,000 Swiss pikemen, 600 archers, and 1,000 artillerymen. The Venetians mustered 25,000, including 2,000 *stradiots* (Balkan mercenaries), under the command of Francesco Gonzaga. His plan was to attack the right flank of the French column with the bulk of his forces, while the *stradiots* harried the left. But at the Battle of Fornovo, the latter turned to plunder instead and the Swiss were able to drive off the Venetians, allowing the French Army to escape. Gonzaga himself was killed at the height of the battle.

REDCOAT VICTORY AT HUBBARDTON

In the Saratoga Campaign of 1777, during the American Revolutionary War, several engagements were fought to slow down the advance of General Burgoyne's British Army invading from Canada. Hubbardton, Vermont, saw one such action.

General Arthur St. Clair evacuated Fort Ticonderoga on July 5, withdrawing south in the face of Burgoyne's army. But his assistant, General Simon Fraser, caught up with the Americans at Hubbardton on July 7. In a hard-fought battle, 1,200 Continentals were defeated by 1,000 Redcoats, 41 being killed and over 200 captured. But the bulk of St. Clair's army was able to escape farther south along the Hudson.

ALSO ON THIS DAY

1520

Spanish conquistadors fight a large Aztec army on the plain of Otumba, resulting in 500 Spaniards defeating 20,000 Aztecs thanks to their repeated cavalry attacks.

JULY

1709

PETER THE GREAT'S RUSSIA COMES OF AGE

The Battle of Poltava is one of the decisive battles of history because it marked the beginning of the ascendancy of Russian power in Eastern Europe.

The Swedish King Charles XII had laid siege to the city of Poltava, Ukraine, in May 1709, with 20,000 troops and 3,000 Cossacks. In June, Tsar Peter I marched to its relief with 60,000 troops, establishing counter-siege lines of entrenchments and artillery.

Charles ordered an attack on the Russian positions, sustaining numerous Swedish casualties and failing to capture his objectives. After two hours of battle, Peter launched a counterattack, pushing the Swedes back into a narrow strip formed by the Vorskla and Dnieper rivers. The entire Swedish Army was either killed or captured, though Charles himself escaped. Swedish power was forever broken.

The Battle of Poltava is one of the decisive battles of history because it marked the beginning of the ascendancy of Russian power in Eastern Europe.

JULY

1386

COMMON FOOT SOLDIERS DEFEAT HAPSBURG KNIGHTS

At the Battle of Sempach, in Lucerne in central Switzerland, 8,000 Swiss foot soldiers armed with halberds defeated 4,000 knights led by Leopold III of Austria.

The two armies encountered each other on a road, Leopold ordering his knights to dismount and fight on foot with their lances to counter the Swiss halberds (a wooden shaft with a blade that had an ax on one side, a pick on the other, and a spike on the end). The knights initially pushed the Swiss back, but the latter were able to maneuver and assault the Austrian left-rear, causing the knights to rout. Leopold lost 1,500 men and his own life. The Swiss lost 200 men.

ALSO ON THIS DAY

1745

The French defeat an Allied army at the Battle of Melle in Flanders, during the War of the Austrian Succession. Around 500 Allies are killed and 1,500 captured.

1645

ROYALIST DEFEAT IN THE WEST

By July 1645, Royalist fortunes in the English Civil War were at a low ebb. King Charles I had been defeated at the Battle of Naseby in June, which allowed the Parliament's New Model Army, commanded by General Thomas Fairfax, to march to relieve Taunton in the southwest of England, which had been besieged by Royalist forces under George, Lord Goring.

Goring's 7,000 men took up a position on a ridge one mile (1.6 km) east of the small town of Langport, Somerset, in front of which was a stream with a ford. Goring positioned two cannons to cover the ford and lined the hedges behind with musketeers. His plan was adequate, but the New Model Army was a battle-hardened force and when Fairfax arrived, he sent Thomas Rainsborough with 1,500 musketeers to clear the hedges, which they did.

Fairfax next sent two divisions of cavalry to deal with the Royalist horsemen on top of the ridge. The Cavaliers managed a counterattack before they fled, pursued by the Roundhead cavalry (and harried by locals whom Goring's soldiers had plundered in the weeks beforehand). The Battle of Langport was one of the final nails in the Royalist coffin.

1708

MARLBOROUGH'S MASTERPIECE AT OUDENARDE

During the War of the Spanish Succession, Louis XIV of France sent Marshal Vendôme and 100,000 men to reoccupy Flanders. In response, John Churchill, Duke of Marlborough, left Brussels with 80,000 English, Dutch, and German troops, crossing the Scheldt River on July 11, below the city of Oudenarde, after having marched 50 miles (80 km) in 65 hours.

Before Vendôme could deploy properly, Marlborough sent his right flank, under Prince Eugene of Savoy, against Vendôme's left. Marlborough himself commanded the Allied center, while sending Dutch troops under Marshal Overkirk wide to the left to attack the French right flank. These moves resulted in the Allied flanks trapping almost half the French Army by sundown.

The Battle of Oudenarde cost the French 6,000 killed or wounded and more than 7,000 captured. Marlborough suffered 3,000 casualties and had restored the Allies' initiative in Flanders. He had taken a huge risk by crossing his whole army over a major river in the proximity of the enemy, but his calculated gamble paid off. Marlborough's friend and fellow commander, Prince Eugene, who was an excellent commander in his own right, also complemented Marlborough brilliantly.

JULY 12 1943

ALLIED NAVAL DEFEAT IN THE SOLOMON ISLANDS

During July 1943, a Japanese naval task force of ten ships was sailing down "The Slot" from the upper Solomons to the island of Kolombangara to disembark troops. On the night of July 12/13, it was intercepted by U.S. Task Force 18, commanded by Rear Admiral Ainsworth. In the resulting Battle of Kolombangara, the U.S. Navy lost one destroyer sunk and three light cruisers heavily damaged, for one Japanese light cruiser sunk. The Japanese were able to land their troops on the island, though the Japanese naval commander, Vice Admiral Izaki, was killed during the battle.

▼ U.S. Navy sailors stand atop the U.S.S. *Honolulu* after it was damaged in the Battle of Kolombangara, in Tulagi, Soloman Islands.

JULY 13 982

A CLASH OF CIVILIZATIONS AT STILO

The Holy Roman Emperor Otto II led a great army of predominantly Germans against the Muslim army of Abu'l-Qasim, Emir of Sicily. The two forces clashed at Stilo, southern Italy. The battle began well for Otto, his German horsemen smashing into the center of the Muslim force and killing Abu'l-Qasim. But the Muslims, roused to fury, counterattacked and routed Otto's army, 4,000 of his soldiers being killed. The emperor himself escaped north to Verona, but the Holy Roman Empire had suffered a major defeat, which sparked rebellions throughout its domains. For example, the Liutzi, one of the Slavic tribes living east of the River Elbe, rose in revolt after hearing of the defeat at Stilo. They destroyed the bishoprics of Brandenburg and Havelburg and then crossed the Elbe to wreak havoc in Saxon territory.

The emperor himself escaped north to Verona, but the Holy Roman Empire had suffered a major defeat.

JULY 14 1864

REBEL DEFEAT IN MISSISSIPPI

In the Battle of Tupelo during the American Civil War, Nathan Bedford Forrest's Confederate troops were defeated by a much larger force of 14,000 Union troops commanded by General Andrew J. Smith.

The attacks were poorly coordinated and after three hours of fighting had failed to breach the Union lines.

Forrest, in conjunction with General Stephen Lee, attacked Smith's troops dug in around Tupelo, Mississippi, the Confederates having to advance uphill across nearly a mile (1.6 km) of open ground. But the attacks were poorly coordinated and after three hours of fighting had failed to breach the Union lines. The Confederates lost more than 1,300 men to Union losses of 674. But Smith missed an opportunity to destroy Forrest and Lee when he failed to launch a counterattack.

JULY 15 1410

DEATH OF THE TEUTONIC KNIGHTS AT TANNENBERG

For 400 years the Teutonic Knights had been elite warriors, the backbone of Christian armies in the Middle East and subsequently in Eastern Europe. But at the Battle of Tannenberg, their power was broken forever.

The knights had ruled northern Poland with an iron hand, provoking a rebellion led by King Władysław Jagiełło, Grand Duke of Lithuania and King of Poland. Władysław raised an army of 20,000 and met the Teutonic army at Tannenberg, a village in northern Poland. The subsequent battle routed the Teutonic Knights, their grand master being killed along with thousands of his men. The Teutonic Order never recovered from this defeat.

▶ Painting of the *Battle of Grunwald*, the First Battle of Tannenberg, by Jan Matejko.

JULY 16
1212

LAS NAVAS DE TOLOSA: RECOVERING SPAIN FROM THE MUSLIMS

Following his 1195 defeat at the Battle of Alarcos, King Alfonso VIII of Castile formed an alliance with the kings of Aragon and Navarre against the Berber Caliph al-Nasir.

At the Battle of Las Navas de Tolosa in Andalusia, the Muslim army's defensive field fortification was successfully assaulted by heavily armored Spanish cavalry and infantry. The Moorish infantry defended a rampart constructed of large earth-filled baskets, with a ditch in front. Spearmen stood in the front rank with archers and javelin-throwers behind. Cavalry formed a reserve. Though the caliph's army was large (up to 30,000), many of the men had had no pay and were mutinous.

The Spanish, numbering up to 14,000, well equipped and with good morale, attacked with their horsemen in front and disciplined infantry closely following. When the Christian soldiers reached the field fortifications the caliph lost his nerve and ordered a retreat. Al-Nasir fled to North Africa where he was assassinated.

The battle was a pivotal clash of the *Reconquista*, the defeat and expulsion of the Moors from Spain between the 9th and 15th centuries.

▼ Spanish Christians fight the Muslim army at the Battle of Las Navas de Tolosa.

JULY

1453

THE END OF THE HUNDRED YEARS' WAR

The Battle of Castillon, fought on this day in 1453, signaled the end of the Hundred Years' War between England and France.

In 1452, Sir John Talbot had led a small army of 6,000 and recaptured Bordeaux. The next year, around 10,000 French soldiers under Jean de Bueil advanced to the town of Castillon, on the lower Dordogne, southwest France, as a counter. Once there, the French master gunner Jean Bureau (who had directed the cannon in no less than 60 sieges between 1449 and 1450) supervised the construction of a large artillery camp, 700 yards (640 m) long and 200 yards (183 m) wide, inside which were no fewer than 300 cannon.

Talbot saw the camp as a tempting target and attacked it with 6,000 men. The French camp, protected on three sides by a ditch and palisaded rampart, was a formidable position, however. When the English attacked, it was literally bristling with guns. But Talbot believed the fury of an attack would win the day. He was wrong. Under a withering artillery fire, the English managed to reach the breastworks but were pushed back. Then French cavalry appeared on the English right flank. Talbot's army dissolved into a rout. English losses were 4,000 dead, wounded, or captured. Talbot himself lay dead on the field.

JULY

1702

SWEDISH DEFEAT AT HUMMELSHOF

The brilliant, erratic King Charles XII of Sweden won many battles, but ultimately led his country to defeat and financial ruin. The cost of fighting a war against Poland, Denmark, and Russia was beyond the resources of Sweden, and military defeats merely exacerbated the strain on the Swedish treasury.

One such defeat occurred during the Great Northern War, when 30,000 Russian soldiers led by Marshal Boris Sheremetev overcame 8,000 Swedes, commanded by General von Schlippenbach, at Hummelshof in Swedish Livonia. Half of the Swedish army was killed or wounded.

ALSO ON THIS DAY

390BC

The Senones, one of the Gallic tribes, defeat the Romans at the Battle of the Allia during the invasion of Italy, 11 miles (16 km) north of Rome. Afterwards, the Gauls sack the city.

JULY

1972

WHO DARES WINS: NINE SAS SOLDIERS TAKE ON AN ARMY

In 1972, the kingdom of Oman was threatened by Communist guerrillas. Britain was an ally of Oman and sent army teams to the country to ensure it did not fall. One such team was a nine-man detachment from 8 Troop, B Squadron, 22 SAS (Special Air Service), which was garrisoning two old forts at Mirbat, along with 25 Omani gendarmes and 30 tribesmen. They were attacked by 300 Communist guerrillas armed with automatic rifles and recoilless rifles.

The SAS soldiers and their allies fought all day, firing an old 25-pounder field gun at waves of attacking guerrillas. Two SAS soldiers were killed but the forts held out until Omani jets arrived to pepper the guerrillas with cannon fire. The Battle of Mirbat was a turning point in the war against the Communist guerrillas, which ended in 1975.

The Battle of Mirbat was a turning point in the war against the Communist guerrillas, which ended in 1975.

JULY

1402

TAMERLANE CAPTURES AN OTTOMAN SULTAN AT ANGORA

Tamerlane invaded Asia Minor in 1402, forcing Bayezid I to abandon his siege of Constantinople.

Tamerlane, or Timur, the great Turco-Mongol warlord (1335–1405), invaded Asia Minor in 1402, forcing the Ottoman Sultan Bayezid I to abandon his siege of Constantinople and face Tamerlane in Anatolia. With his army reinforced by Christian troops, Bayezid reached Angora in Anatolia (present-day Ankara, Turkey). He had some 85,000 troops, a fourth of whom were Crimean Tatars. Tamerlane's army was comprised mainly of Turco-Mongolian light cavalry, with some heavy cavalry and 32 war elephants.

The Ottomans attacked but were stopped by Tatar arrows and naphtha, both flanks being defeated. Tamerlane then attacked Bayezid's center, using the elephants to pin them. The Ottoman army collapsed, some 40,000 troops perishing in the defeat. Bayezid was taken and died in captivity.

JULY 21 1798

NAPOLEON: MASTER OF THE LEVANT

After driving Austrian armies out of Italy, Napoleon decided to strike at the British in India by way of Egypt, landing west of Alexandria with 30,000 troops at the beginning of July 1798.

The Mameluke ruler, Ibrahim Bey, fled to the east of the Nile. But the Mameluke military commander, Murad Bey, blocked the French advance toward Cairo by holding Embabeh, north of the Pyramids, on the left bank of the Nile. He fought Napoleon on July 21, his army numbering 40,000 men (though only his Mameluke cavalry could be termed reliable soldiers, the rest being ill-trained levies). He launched his 6,000 Mameluke cavalry against the French, who formed squares and shot the horsemen to pieces with musket and artillery fire, while a French flanking force captured Embabeh. Up to 3,000 Mameluke cavalrymen were killed and hundreds of infantry drowned in the Nile. The Battle of the Pyramids cost Napoleon 29 soldiers.

▼ *The Battle of the Pyramids* by Louis-François, Baron Lejeune.

WELLINGTON'S GREAT VICTORY AT SALAMANCA

Following Wellington's capture of the city of Salamanca, Spain, the French marshal Marmont (50,000 men and 78 guns) attacked the duke's army south of the city on July 22. Wellington (48,500 men and 60 guns) reordered his army to face south as well as east, launching an attack against the French left flank that shattered a fourth of Marmont's army. The marshal himself was injured and replaced by General Clauzel, who launched a counterattack that almost broke through Wellington's center, only to be repulsed by the 6th Division.

The failure of this attack broke the morale of the French Army, which streamed away from the battlefield. They had lost 14,000 men to Wellington's 5,200. Victory at the Battle of Salamanca resulted in the duke entering Madrid, which the French had evacuated, on August 12.

The failure of this attack broke the morale of the French Army, which streamed away from the battlefield.

THE HOSPITALLER FLEET TRIUMPHS OVER THE TURKS

The military crusading order the Knights Hospitaller was unusual in having its own warships. By the beginning of the 14th century they had a fleet of galleys operating from Rhodes (they had first sought sanctuary on Cyprus after the loss of the Holy Land but found the island's politics undesirable). The principal enemy of the Hospitallers were the Turks, whose ships carried out piracy in the Aegean Sea.

On this day, a fleet of 24 Hospitaller galleys met and defeated a Turkish fleet of 18 galleys and 18 other vessels off the island of Chios in the Aegean. The Christians sank or captured all but six of the Turkish vessels.

ALSO ON THIS DAY

1916

The Battle of Pozières, part of the huge Battle of the Somme, begins on the Western Front in World War I. It ends on September 3, by which time Australian and New Zealand losses total 23,000.

JULY 24 1848

ITALIAN FREEDOM IS SMASHED AT CUSTOZA

By the middle of the 19th century, Italy was divided into a number of states, most of which were dominated by the Austrian Empire. This caused resentment against the Austrians, coming to a head in Milan, Lombardy, in March 1848 during the so-called "Five Days of Milan." Field Marshal Joseph Radetzky's Austrian Army was expelled from Milan, King Charles Albert of Sardinia–Piedmont declared support for the Milanese, and Venice declared its independence from Austria. The First Italian War of Independence had begun.

Charles declared war on Austria, fancying himself as a modern-day Caesar, and his Piedmontese Army of 22,000 men moved to intercept and destroy the Austrians. Charles' soldiers and other Italian rebels fought Radetzky's army of 33,000 troops at Custoza, 11 miles (18 km) southwest of Verona, on July 24.

The battle initially went well for the Italians but on the 25th the Austrians counterattacked and drove Charles out of Lombardy. Radetzky had dealt a huge blow to Italian independence.

JULY 25 1814

A BLOODY BATTLE NEAR NIAGARA FALLS After five hours of combat, the Americans withdrew from the bloody Battle of Lundy's Lane, part of the 1812 Anglo-American War.

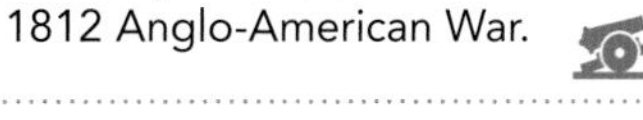

JULY 26 657

THREE-DAY BATTLE IN THE MUSLIM CIVIL WAR The battle between Ali ibn Abi Talib and Muawiyah began at Siffin in Syria, resulting in a victory for the former.

JULY 27 1214

ICONIC FRENCH VICTORY King Philip Augustus of France defeated an Anglo-Flemish-German army at Bouvines in Flanders, in one of France's most iconic battles.

JULY 28 1809

BRITISH VICTORY IN SPAIN Arthur Wellesley was created Viscount Wellington after his triumph over King Joseph Bonaparte at Talavera, southwest of Madrid, Spain.

JULY 29 1693

FRENCH CRUSH WILLIAM III English King William III was defeated by French marshal Duc de Luxembourg at Neerwinden (in present-day Belgium).

JULY 30 1864

DISASTER IN THE CRATER During the siege of Petersburg in the American Civil War, a mine of explosives broke the Confederate line but the later Union attack failed.

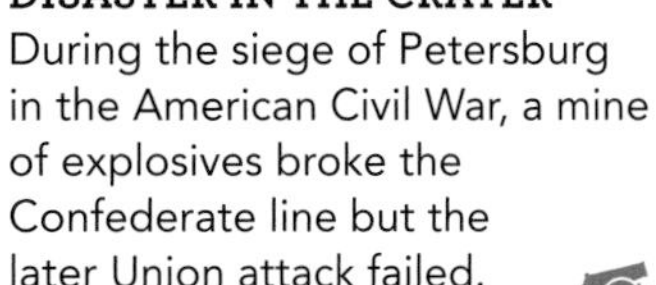

JULY 31 1423

SCOTTISH DEFEAT An army of 4,000 Anglo-Burgundians defeated a Scottish–French force of 8,000 at Cravant in Burgundy during the Hundred Years' War.

CHAPTER 8

August

1759

ANGLO-GERMAN SUCCESS AGAINST THE FRENCH AT MINDEN

The Seven Years' War was a global conflict between a British-led coalition on one side and France, Russia, Spain, and Sweden on the other. The Battle of Minden was fought to prevent the French from taking Hanover.

The Anglo-German army under the command of the Duke of Brunswick had been forced to retire deep into Westphalia by the French capture of the town of Minden in Hanover. Determined to clear the French from Hanover, the duke marched toward Minden, to find the French drawn up in strong positions in front of the town, between the Weser River and Minden marsh. Worse, the French commander, the Marquis de Contades, had 48,000 troops to Brunswick's 38,000 (though Brunswick had 187 cannon to Contades' 162).

The battle began with what should have been a disaster for Brunswick when six of his British and three of his Hanoverian infantry battalions attacked 60 squadrons of cavalry deployed in the center of the French line. The horsemen charged the infantry three times, to be repulsed each time by well-aimed volley fire. Then 37 squadrons of Allied cavalry charged and routed the French right wing, after which Contades ordered a retreat. The French had 7,000 killed, wounded, or missing men, and Hanover had been wrested from their grasp.

▲ The Allied army commanded by Prince Ferdinand of Brunswick-Wolfenbüttel was victorious at the Battle of Minden.

216 BCE

HANNIBAL'S MASTERPIECE AT CANNAE

The Carthaginian general Hannibal is one of the "great captains" of history. His place in the pantheon of military legends was cemented by his victory over the Romans at the Battle of Cannae in southern Italy.

Hannibal, having led a Carthaginian army over the Alps in 218 BCE, was campaigning in Italy. Rome sent two consuls, Gaius Terentius Varro and Lucius Aemilius Paullus, and an army of 80,000 men to confront him in a decisive battle. The site for the clash was on a narrow plain beside the Aufidus (present-day Ofanto) River, below the town of Cannae. The Roman position was strong, having hills on the left and the river on the right, so Hannibal's cavalry would be unable to outflank it. The consuls arrayed their army with the infantry in the center and cavalry on both wings.

Hannibal deployed his 50,000 men in a convex shape, also with his cavalry on the wings and infantry in the center. When the Romans attacked, the Carthaginian center was pushed back into a concave shape, as Hannibal had planned. As the Roman soldiers became packed into the salient, the heavy cavalry on Hannibal's left flank defeated the Roman horsemen on both wings, before completing the encirclement of the entire Roman Army. It was their heaviest defeat with 50,000 deaths.

1645

COSTLY VICTORY FOR THE FRENCH AT NÖRDLINGEN

In the final phase of the Thirty Years' War (1618–48), France and her allies had pushed back the Imperialists on all fronts, though suffering the occasional reverse. By 1645 they were in Bavaria where 12,000 troops under Louis II de Bourbon (subsequently Prince de Condé) engaged a similar number of Imperialists, commanded by Field Marshal von Mercy, at Nördlingen, Bavaria.

The Imperial army fought well, but von Mercy was mortally wounded at the height of the battle and with his fall his men began to lose ground, being driven back to the Danube with losses of more than 5,000. The French, suffering similar losses, were too crippled to pursue.

Nördlingen is a perfect example of the final phase of the Thirty Years' War, in which French armies, at first incapable of achieving decisive victories against Spanish and Imperialist forces, gradually achieved military superiority over the armies of Emperor Ferdinand III.

The French, suffering similar losses, were too crippled to pursue.

DEATH OF SIMON DE MONTFORT AT EVESHAM

The Second Barons' War of 1264–67 was initiated by a group of English barons led by Simon de Montfort, Earl of Leicester, against King Henry III. They had defeated the royalists and captured the king at the Battle of Lewes in Sussex in 1264, but the following year de Montfort was soundly defeated at the Battle of Evesham in Worcestershire. Montfort and his son Henry were killed at the battle, along with 4,000 of their soldiers. Henry III was rescued and restored to the throne, ruling until 1272.

English barons led the battle against Henry III.

◀ Henry III, who had been de Montfort's prisoner, stumbles through the Battle of Evesham, wounded and confused.

1716

STEMMING THE OTTOMAN TIDE AT PETERWARDEIN

The defeat of Ottoman forces before the gates of Vienna in 1683 did not stop Turkish incursions into Christian Europe. In 1716, Prince Eugene of Savoy, acting on behalf of Charles VI, Holy Roman Emperor, marched into the Balkans with an army of 40,000 men. Eugene and many of his men were veterans of the War of the Spanish Succession, which was just as well, since at Peterwardein (now Petrovaradin), on the Danube in Serbia, he encountered 100,000 Turkish troops under the command of Grand Vizier Silahdar Damat Ali Pasha.

Eugene joined with the Serb garrison of 8,000 and attacked the Ottoman Army besieging Peterwardein. Eugene himself led the attack on the Grand Vizier's encampment, which was supported by cannon from Austrian frigates on the Danube. After seven hours of fighting, the Grand Vizier was dead along with half his army. The rest of the Ottoman force returned to Belgrade.

The Austrians lost 3,000 men in the battle, the Ottomans twice that number. They also lost 172 artillery pieces captured by the Austrians, plus their camp.

1623

END OF THE PALATINE PHASE OF THE THIRTY YEARS' WAR Count Tilly of the Catholic League defeated the Protestant Christian of Brunswick at Stadtlohn.

1819

BOLÍVAR DEFEATS THE SPANISH AT BOYACÁ Simón Bolívar defeated the Spanish at Boyacá in the decisive battle of the Colombian War of Independence.

1588

DAMAGE TO SPANISH SHIPS The battle between English ships and the Spanish Armada at Gravelines, near Dunkirk, led the Spanish ships to suffer heavy damage.

378

EMPEROR VALENS IS KILLED The Roman emperor Valens and two-thirds of his army were killed after defeat at Adrianople (now Edirne in Turkey) by an army of barbarian Visigoths.

1557

SPANISH VICTORY During the Hapsburg–Valois War, a French army attempting to relieve the besieged town of Saint-Quentin was defeated by a Spanish army.

991

EPIC BATTLE IN ESSEX The defeat of Earl Byrhtnoth's East Saxons by Danish Vikings under Olaf Tryggvason on August 11 is told in the Anglo-Saxon poem *The Battle of Maldon.*

1099

HOLY LAND DEFEAT An army of Egyptian Muslims was defeated by Norman knights at Ascalon in the Holy Land (now Ashkelon, Israel) during the First Crusade.

1708

MARLBOROUGH: MASTER OF WAR

John Churchill, First Duke of Marlborough, was one of Britain's greatest soldiers, whose victories during the War of the Spanish Succession established the British Army as a premier fighting force.

In 1704, a French attempt to capture Vienna resulted in Marshal Tallard's Franco-Bavarian army appearing north of the Danube in Bavaria, threatening the line of communications for Marlborough. With his trusted lieutenant, Prince Eugene of Savoy, Marlborough decided to move north of the Danube to engage in battle near the village of Blenheim (Blindheim in German).

Despite being outnumbered by 56,000 to 52,000, Marlborough's tactical skill led to victory. Tallard fought on the defensive, believing the garrisons of Blenheim and the village of Oberglau would attack the Allied flanks and lure Marlborough into making a costly frontal attack against the French center. But Marlborough contained the French strongpoints, Eugene on his right flank battling the Bavarians.

In the late afternoon, Marlborough unleashed 80 squadrons of cavalry and 23 battalions of infantry against Tallard's weakened center, routing the French troops and winning the battle. For the loss of 12,500 casualties, Marlborough had inflicted a major defeat on the French, with 21,000 casualties and 14,000 taken prisoner, including Tallard himself.

1914

FRENCH CALAMITY IN LORRAINE IN WORLD WAR I

Having lost Alsace and Lorraine in the Franco-Prussian War, when World War I began, France sent troops into these regions to recapture them from the Germans. The Battle of Lorraine began well for the French 1st and 2nd Armies, the German 6th and 7th Armies retreating before them. But the German commander, Crown Prince Rupprecht of Bavaria, was merely luring the French into heavily defended positions where they were subjected to intense machine-gun and artillery fire. The Germans then launched a counterattack that overwhelmed the French divisions, which by August 25 had been pushed back to their starting positions.

▼ The German artillery advance in Alsace-Lorraine, in August 1914.

1760

FREDERICK THE GREAT TRIUMPHS AGAINST ALL ODDS AT LIEGNITZ

During the Seven Years' War, Frederick the Great of Prussia found himself in danger of being trapped by 90,000 Austrian and Russian troops that were closing in on him. In desperation, he tried to slip through the trap. But his 30,000 Prussians ran into 25,000 Austrian soldiers, commanded by General von Laudon, near the Silesian town of Liegnitz (now Legnica in Poland).

An Austrian cavalry attack was repulsed by Prussian hussars, after which an artillery duel also went the way of the Prussians. The Prussian artillery then repulsed an Austrian infantry attack. The battle was decided when the highly trained Prussian infantry attacked and forced the Austrians to retreat. For the loss of 3,400 dead and wounded, Frederick escaped from the Allied trap. Austrian losses were 10,000 killed, wounded, and captured.

Frederick the Great of Prussia found himself in danger of being trapped by 90,000 Austrian and Russian troops.

1920

POLAND SAVES WESTERN EUROPE

The Battle of Warsaw in August 1920 was a turning point in European history, saving as it did both Poland and Germany from Communist revolutions.

The triumph of the Bolsheviks in the Russian Civil War resulted in the Red Army launching an offensive against the Ukrainians and Poles in May 1920, Soviet troops under the command of Marshal Tukhachevsky overwhelming the Poles and Ukrainians and driving deep into Poland. By the beginning of August, the Red Army was threatening Warsaw itself. But in Marshal Józef Piłsudski the Poles had a commander capable of halting the Red onslaught.

On August 16, Piłsudski's 20,000-strong assault group spearheaded a Polish counterattack from the south (he had taken men from Warsaw's defenses to reinforce the attacking force), shattering the Soviet line and forcing the Red Army into a hurried retreat. The Russians saw 10,000 killed and 66,000 taken prisoner, Polish losses were 4,500 killed, 10,000 missing, and 22,000 wounded (total Soviet losses during the war are estimated at 100,000 dead). In the space of a few days the Bolshevik Revolution had been halted and then reversed at the gates of Warsaw.

1424

ENGLISH VICTORY AT VERNEUIL

The Battle of Verneuil in Normandy, during the Hundred Years' War, has been described as a second Agincourt. An English army of 8,000 men-at-arms and 1,000 archers, commanded by John, Duke of Bedford, engaged a French force under the Count of Aumale, commanding 15,000 men, including 6,000 Scots and 500 Italian cavalry.

The battle was fought on hard ground north of the town, which made it difficult for the archers to drive in their defensive stakes. Bedford dismounted his men-at-arms and formed them into two "battles," which fought a bloody mêlée with the French, driving them off before surrounding the Scots and slaughtering them. French casualties were up to 8,000 dead; English losses were 1,600.

ALSO ON THIS DAY

1549

English rebels are defeated by royalist troops of King Edward VI at the Battle of Sampford Courtenay in Devon, during the so-called Prayer Book Rebellion.

1870

MISSED OPPORTUNITY AT GRAVELOTTE–SAINT-PRIVAT

During the Franco-Prussian War in 1870, Marshal Bazaine's French army of 150,000 men made a stand west of Metz at Gravelotte, his right flank holding Saint-Privat to the north. On August 18, 1870, the Prussian 1st and 2nd Armies (combined strength 900,000) attacked Bazaine's army.

The French repulsed the Prussian 1st Army at Gravelotte and inflicted heavy casualties on the 2nd Army at Saint-Privat, though the arrival of reinforcements forced the French to withdraw from the town. Nevertheless, the Prussians had lost 20,000 men during the battle, and a French counterattack might have won a decisive victory. But instead, Bazaine withdrew his army into Metz, to be contained by the Prussians.

The French repulsed the Prussian 1st Army at Gravelotte and inflicted heavy casualties on the 2nd Army at Saint-Privat.

1942

DISASTER AT DIEPPE

The British raid on the French port of Dieppe in World War II, codenamed Operation Jubilee, was a disaster that could have been averted with proper prior planning. In what was designed as a trial beach landing, intelligence had failed to notice German gun positions dug into the side of cliffs, no detailed research had been done on the beach gradient and its suitability for tanks, and French double agents had alerted the Germans to British interest in Dieppe.

The amphibious assault was mounted with over 6,000 men—5,000 Canadians and 1,000 British troops and 50 U.S. Rangers. Resistance was heavy from the beginning, the Royal Regiment of Canada being wiped out, for example—only 60 out of 543 were extracted from the beach. Most of the 27 Churchill tanks that landed either got bogged down on the shingle beach or were stopped by concrete roadblocks, to be knocked out by German anti-tank guns. Crossfire from machine-gun posts inflicted heavy casualties on the Allied troops.

With the landings having failed and the troops pinned down by murderous small-arms and artillery fire, an evacuation was ordered. It was completed by 14:00 hours. Some 3,367 Canadians had been killed, wounded, or taken prisoner, the British losing 275 commandos and their Royal Navy losing 550 dead and wounded.

480BCE

SPARTAN HEROISM AT THERMOPYLAE

The last stand of the Spartans at the Battle of Thermopylae is the stuff of military legend and led to the rest of Greece turning back the Persian invaders, saving mainland Europe from Asiatic domination.

King Leonidas of Sparta, his hoplites (spearmen), and archers occupied the defile at Thermopylae—the perfect defensive position against King of Kings Xerxes I and his 200,000 Persian soldiers.

Leonidas deployed 1,000 men in the mountains on his left (his right was protected by the sea) and defended a narrow part of the path, known as the Middle Gate, with 6,000 men. His Spartans and the other Greek hoplites defeated a succession of Persian attacks for three days before a Greek traitor informed Xerxes of a track across the mountains behind Thermopylae. Xerxes' famed Immortals went to take advantage of this intelligence, wiping out the mountain force and appearing behind the Greek position, leaving Leonidas and his remaining hoplites in a hopeless position. They withdrew to a small hill behind the Middle Gate and were offered the chance to surrender, the Persian officer stating that Xerxes had so many archers that when they shot, their arrows would block out the sun. Leonidas replied: "Then we shall fight in the shade." He and his men were then wiped out by arrows.

HELL'S POINT: BATTLE OF THE TENARU RIVER

During World War II, in response to U.S. Marines landing on the island of Guadalcanal in the Solomon Islands in 1942, the Japanese dispatched 900 soldiers of the 28th Infantry Regiment to wipe them out. The Japanese Army had enjoyed a string of victories in the Pacific and were undaunted by the arrival of the 1st U.S. Marine Regiment.

The marines dug in around the mouth of Alligator Creek and waited for the Japanese to attack, which they did at 04:00 hours on August 21. By dawn the fighting at Hell's Point was over. More than 700 Japanese lay dead in front of the marines' positions: U.S. casualties were 37.

▼ U.S. Marines, with full battle kits, charge ashore on Guadalcanal Island, from a landing craft, during the early phase of the U.S. offensive in the Solomon Islands.

1485

BIRTH OF THE TUDOR DYNASTY ON BOSWORTH FIELD

The Battle of Bosworth established the Tudor dynasty. The Lancastrian Henry Tudor, having recruited supporters in France, landed in Wales and marched east, gathering an army of 5,000 as he did so. The Yorkist King Richard III, meanwhile, moved to intercept him with 10,000 men (plus a further 6,000 under Thomas, Lord Stanley, and his brother Sir William). The two forces met south of the village of Market Bosworth in Leicestershire.

Richard may have had the numbers, but the Stanleys proved unreliable, as did the Earl of Northumberland when the battle started. When both sides were locked in combat, Northumberland held back from the fray, while the Stanleys changed sides to join Henry. The Yorkists were overwhelmed, Richard was killed, and Henry Tudor became King Henry VII.

The battle was fought on and around Ambion Hill, close to Sutton Cheney, and lasted for only two hours. Richard had had the best position but had failed to take advantage of it.

The battle lasted for only two hours.

▲ The Yorkist King Richard III of England is killed on Bosworth Field.

THE BLOODING OF THE BEF

During World War I, British troops fought on European soil for the first time since Waterloo when the British Expeditionary Force (BEF) faced the German 1st Army at the Battle of Mons, Belgium.

Though outnumbered, the British troops in the salient formed by a loop in the Mons Canal stood firm for six hours in the face of infantry and artillery assaults. However, the decision by the commander of the French 5th Army, General Lanrezac, to order a general retreat led to a danger of the BEF being enveloped. The BEF's commander, Sir John French, therefore had no option but to retire.

Mons cost the BEF 1,600 casualties out of 35,000 committed. Kaiser Wilhelm of Germany is said to have dubbed the BEF a "contemptible little army," leading to British soldiers afterward branding themselves "the old contemptibles."

▼ The British Expeditionary Force arrives in Belgium ahead of the Battle of Mons.

AUGUST 24

1516

OTTOMAN VICTORY AT MARJ DABIQ

By the beginning of the 16th century, the Ottoman Empire was the major power in the Middle East. When Selim I, the Grim, marched an Ottoman army toward the Euphrates River in 1516, intent on conquering Persia, he was intercepted by an Egyptian Mameluke force, commanded by Kansu al-Gauri, an ally of the Persian shah, Ismail I.

The two armies clashed at the Battle of Marj Dabiq (north of Aleppo in Syria). Ottoman superiority in tactics and artillery crushed the Egyptians, Kansu falling in battle. The Ottomans then seized all of Syria, before marching toward the Nile.

ALSO ON THIS DAY

1914

The World War I Battle of Cer, fought between the Austro-Hungarians and the Serbians, comes to an end. The Serbs have achieved a stunning victory, inflicting 37,000 casualties on the Austrians for just 18,000 of their own.

AUGUST 25

1689

ALLIED VICTORY AGAINST THE FRENCH AT WALCOURT

The expansionist dreams of King Louis XIV of France plunged Europe into war in the late 17th and early 18th centuries as a succession of coalitions sought to curb Louis' ambitions.

The Battle of Walcourt, during the Nine Years' War (1688–97), saw an Allied army, commanded by the Prince of Waldeck, defeat a French army led by Louis de Crevant near Walcourt in the Spanish Netherlands. The battle, in which 35,000 Allies fought 24,000 Frenchmen, is notable for the distinguished actions of the British commander John Churchill, later Duke of Marlborough.

Walcourt was the first battle between English and French forces in the Nine Years' War and, thanks to Churchill's efforts to improve training, demonstrated that the English Army was a force to be reckoned with.

◀ After John Churchill's actions at Walcourt, he became Duke of Marlborough. He is pictured here at the later Battle of Blenheim.

1346

TRIUMPH OF THE ENGLISH LONGBOW AT CRÉCY

In the summer of 1346, during the Hundred Years' War, King Edward II of England was being hounded in northern France by Philip VI. He made his stand at Crécy, north of the Somme River.

Edward had 10,000 men, including 5,000 archers. Philip had a larger army— 28,000, including 6,000 Genoese crossbowmen. The English deployed their archers in wedge-shaped formations to produce a thicker barrage of arrows. They were also aided by a thunderstorm that soaked the ground, making the job of an attacker harder.

Successive French attacks were beaten off with arrows: first the crossbowmen, followed by cavalry and men-at-arms on foot. By midnight, 12,000 French and Genoese lay dead on the ground. English losses were 250 dead. The longbow had become the master of the battlefield.

King Edward II of England was being hounded in northern France by Philip VI.

1626

DEFEAT FOR THE DANES AT LUTTER

Albrecht von Wallenstein and Count Tilly were two of the main Catholic commanders during the Thirty Years' War, and so King Christian IV of Denmark's plan to defeat the latter in the former's absence made sense. With 20,000 troops, Christian struck south into Saxony. But Wallenstein sent Tilly reinforcements to make the numbers equal, and when the two armies met at the Battle of Lutter, Tilly's superior generalship routed the Danes and their Saxon allies. The battle was a disaster for the Protestant cause, all the German Protestant princes suing for peace afterward.

ALSO ON THIS DAY

1798

Irish rebels, assisted by French troops, defeat English militia at the Battle of Castlebar in County Mayo, during the 1798 Irish Rebellion against British rule.

489

DECLINE OF THE ROMAN EMPIRE IN THE WEST

The days of the famed legions had long passed, and now the defense of Italy was in the hands of so-called *foederati*.

In the 5th century, what remained of the Roman Empire in the West was under continual attack from barbarian tribes. The days of the famed legions had long passed, and now the defense of Italy was in the hands of so-called *foederati* (trusted native tribes). Led by Flavius Odoacer, King of Italy, the *foederati* were defeated by an Ostrogoth army at the Battle of Sontius on this day.

The Ostrogoths were led by Theodoric the Great, who would go on to become King of Italy himself by murdering Odoacer in 493 (after promising to share power with him if he surrendered himself and his troops). Despite his treachery, Theodoric went on to become a good king and brought a period of peace to Italy, which had been unknown for decades. Indeed, the land prospered to such a degree that Italy became a grain-exporting country as opposed to an importing one.

1526

THE OTTOMANS CONQUER HUNGARY

The Ottoman Army of the 16th century was a powerful instrument, particularly its artillery arm. When Suleiman I, the Magnificent, marched at the head of 50,000 troops toward Hungary in August 1526, he was also accompanied by 160 cannon served by highly trained crews.

With his kingdom in danger, Louis II of Hungary assembled an army of 20,000 men and 68 cannon on the Danube River at Mohács, Hungary. The battle of the same name lasted around four hours, at the end of which 10,000 Hungarians lay dead on the ground, including Louis himself. Suleiman went on to capture Budapest.

ALSO ON THIS DAY

1350

At the naval battle of Winchelsea during the Hundred Years' War, 40 English warships defeat a Castilian fleet of 47 larger vessels off East Sussex, England.

CONFEDERATE VICTORY AT SECOND MANASSAS

The Battle of Second Manassas, which concluded on August 30 in Virginia during the American Civil War, resulted from General Lee's desire to deal with the Union Army of Virginia before it could be joined by the Army of the Potomac.

General John Pope, commander of the Army of Virginia, initially had the better of it against "Stonewall" Jackson, but during the afternoon of the 30th the Confederates were reinforced by troops led by General James Longstreet. Pope assaulted Jackson's position, only to be repulsed. Then his army was hit on the left by Longstreet's 28,000 soldiers, which drove Pope's army back to Bull Run.

The three-day battle had cost the Union 13,824 casualties; Confederate losses were 8,353. Lee was now in a position to mount an invasion of the North.

On September 1, the Confederates clashed with Pope again in a bloody battle at Ox Hill—Jackson hoping to cut off the Union retreat. Pope lost a further 1,300 men, Jackson 800. The Union commander went on to order the retreat to continue to Washington.

▼ Company C of the 41st New York Infantry before the Second Battle of Bull Run in Manassas, Virginia.

AUGUST 31

1813

AN EASY VICTORY FOR WELLINGTON AT SAN MARCIAL

In the summer of 1813, the Marquess (later Duke) of Wellington was pushing back his Napoleonic enemies toward the borders of France itself. His British and Spanish troops had the coastal city of San Sebastián under siege, which Marshal Soult was determined to relieve.

The terrain was undulating and the cohesion of the attack soon broke down.

Mustering 18,000 troops, Soult attacked on the morning of August 31 in the locale of San Marcial; but the terrain was undulating and the cohesion of the attack soon broke down, being thrown back down the slope by Spanish troops deployed on the crest of the hill. Soult rallied his men and attempted a second attack up the hill, which was also repulsed by the Spanish troops. The Battle of San Marcial cost the French 4,000 dead or wounded; Spanish losses were 2,500.

▲ Spanish troops triumph over the French at the Battle of San Marcial.

CHAPTER 9

September

1870

SEDAN: A CRUSHING FRENCH DEFEAT

During the Franco-Prussian War of 1870, following Marshal Bazaine's withdrawal with his army into the fortress of Metz, Emperor Napoleon III marched north with 130,000 troops of France's last remaining field army to relieve him. But the Prussians reacted quickly, the Army of the Meuse deflecting Napoleon away from Metz and the 3rd Army forcing him into the border fortress of Sedan on the Meuse River.

On this day, the French tried to fight their way out, but at the Battle of Sedan 3,000 were killed, 14,000 were wounded, and 20,000 were taken prisoner. Prussian losses were 9,000 killed and wounded. Napoleon III surrendered, and on the following day the rest of the French Army gave up, thus ending the French Second Empire.

▼ Otto von Bismarck and Napoleon III meet after the Battle of Sedan.

31 BCE

MARK ANTONY AND CLEOPATRA'S SWANSONG AT ACTIUM

The fate of the Roman world was decided off Akri in western Greece, at the Battle of Actium.

Mark Antony, friend of Julius Caesar and later Roman triumvir, was besotted with the Egyptian Queen Cleopatra VII. Under her influence he had provoked a civil war with the future emperor, Octavian, in Rome, marching to Greece with an army to fight his rival. But Octavian's naval commander, Marcus Agrippa, cut off Antony's supply route by sea. Antony could have retreated, but Cleopatra insisted they return to Egypt by sea. In the resulting sea battle, their 290 ships were defeated by Octavian's 400. Antony's land army surrendered and his allies deserted him. A year later, Antony and Cleopatra committed suicide.

Mark Antony was besotted with the Egyptian Queen Cleopatra VII.

▶ Cleopatra supported Mark Antony at the Battle of Actium.

1650

CROMWELL'S GREAT VICTORY AT DUNBAR

In response to the Scots siding with English King Charles II in early 1650, Oliver Cromwell led an English Parliamentarian army of 15,000 north to invade Scotland. Moving first to secure the port of Dunbar on Scotland's east coast, he then advanced on Edinburgh, but poor weather and a lack of supplies forced him back to Dunbar.

The Scots marched down the hill, which was a tactical mistake.

The Scottish Army of 25,000, commanded by General David Leslie, occupied Doon Hill overlooking the Parliamentarian army at Dunbar, interposing himself between Cromwell and his line of retreat back to Scotland. But on September 3, the Scots marched down the hill, which was a tactical mistake. Cromwell attacked, shattered the Scottish right flank, and then rolled up their center, inflicting 3,000 casualties and taking 10,000 prisoners for the loss of 20 killed and 58 wounded.

1839

FIRST SHOT OF THE OPIUM WAR

The selling of opium to the Chinese led to conflict between the British and Chinese Empires. The spark that triggered the war occurred in Kowloon, which would later become the British port of Hong Kong.

The arrest of a British naval officer, followed by a riot on land by the officer's crew, which led to the death of a Chinese man, eventually produced a standoff in Kowloon harbor between Chinese war junks and three frigates of the Royal Navy. Fighting commenced on this day, the frigates and junks exchanging broadsides, the Chinese supported by shore batteries, all of which achieved very little. But the Chinese commander, Lai Enjue, wrote a report afterward claiming that the Chinese had achieved a great victory.

The selling of opium to the Chinese led to conflict between the British and Chinese empires.

1781

THE BATTLE THAT DECIDED AMERICA'S INDEPENDENCE

In a two-hour battle in Chesapeake Bay, off the coast of Maryland and Virginia, a French fleet of 25 warships, commanded by Admiral Comte de Grasse, defeated a British fleet of 19 ships, commanded by Admiral Thomas Graves.

The battle itself was secondary to the fact that afterward the French were able to position their warships at the mouth of Chesapeake Bay, which prevented the British from reinforcing or evacuating the army of General Cornwallis during the subsequent siege of Yorktown. In addition, the arrival of the siege train aboard the French vessels would make a significant contribution to the surrender of Cornwallis, which would lead the British to sue for peace in the Revolutionary War.

▲ The surrender of British troops led by General Cornwallis at Yorktown, Virginia, on October 20, 1781.

1634

CRUSHING CATHOLIC VICTORY AT NÖRDLINGEN

In 1634, during the Thirty Years' War, the Imperialist Archduke Ferdinand (the future Emperor Ferdinand III) led an army of 15,000 to lay siege to the Swedish-occupied town of Nördlingen, Bavaria. There he was joined by his Spanish cousin, also called Ferdinand, with 18,000 Spanish soldiers. The approach of Sweden's Gustaf Horn with a relief army of 16,000 infantry and 9,000 cavalry, resulted in the First Battle of Nördlingen.

For seven hours Horn tried to capture a hill on the Imperialist left flank. His eventual withdrawal prompted the Imperialists to launch a frontal assault against the Protestants, which shattered Horn's already tired troops. The result was 17,000 Protestant dead and 4,000 captured, including Horn imself.

ALSO ON THIS DAY

1781

During the American Revolutionary War, a British force defeats a smaller Connecticut militia unit at the Battle of Groton Heights.

1191

RICHARD THE LIONHEART TRIUMPHS OVER SALADIN AT ARSUF

England's King Richard the Lionheart was a leading military figure during the Third Crusade. After capturing the port of Acre in August 1191, he moved on to Jaffa, a bridgehead for attacks on Jerusaem (the capture of which was the crusade's purpose). Forming his army of 11,000 men into a defensive column, in which wings of foot soldiers defended the cavalry from Muslim archery and charges, he began his march south. His army was continually harassed by up to 25,000 Muslim horsemen under the command of the Ayubbid Sultan Saladin, the issue being decided on September 7 near the town of Arsuf. Richard kept his infantry and knights under tight control, charging Saladin's forces three times and routing them, after which he continued his advance.

His army was harassed by up to 25,000 Muslim horsemen under the command of the Ayubbid Sultan Saladin.

1855

DECISIVE BATTLE OF THE CRIMEAN WAR

The Russian naval arsenal at Sebastopol was the focal point of the main operations in the Crimean War (1853–6). It was besieged by Anglo-French forces from October 1854, the Russian garrison of 38,000 beating off several half-hearted and poorly planned attacks.

But on September 8, 1855, after a heavy bombardment, French and British troops advanced once more against the Russian defenses, the French taking a key redoubt during the Battle of Malakoff, though suffering 7,567 casualties in four hours of combat as they did so (the British were repulsed). The Russian commander, Prince Gorchakov, abandoned the city the next day, signaling the approaching end of the war.

ALSO ON THIS DAY

1514

A combined Lithuanian–Polish army of 35,000 defeats a larger Muscovite force of 80,000 men at the Battle of Orsha, in the Grand Duchy of Lithuania.

1513

THE LAST GREAT BATTLE WON BY THE ENGLISH LONGBOW

Northumberland seemed set to fall, but Thomas Howard, Earl of Surrey, rallied 25,000 troops and met the Scots at Flodden Field.

In 1513, while English King Henry VIII was fighting the French, a Scottish army of 50,000 under King James IV of Scotland invaded northern England. The county of Northumberland seemed set to fall, but Thomas Howard, Earl of Surrey, rallied 25,000 troops and met the Scots at Flodden Field.

The Scots deployed on a hill to fight a defensive battle, their foot soldiers mustered in *schiltrons* (dense circles of spearmen). Surrey bombarded the Scots with artillery and volleys of arrows shot by his archers. The Scots then charged down the hill, to be cut down by English bills (long poles topped with a curved blade).

1547

VICTORY FOR THE BOY-KING EDWARD VI AT PINKIE CLEUGH

King Henry VIII of England had sought to cement an alliance with Scotland by marrying his young son, Edward, to the equally young Mary, Queen of Scots. The Scots rejected Henry's offer, which led to war between the two countries after Henry's death early in 1547.

The Duke of Somerset, *de facto* lord protector of England, marched north with an army of 18,000, invading Scotland along the east-coast road to Edinburgh. The Scots mustered an army of 22,000 men under the Earl of Arran, who deployed his troops on the west bank of the River Esk to block Somerset's approach to the capital.

The Battle of Pinkie Cleugh (a *cleugh* is a narrow valley in Gaelic) began with an English cavalry charge, which was beaten off by Scottish pikemen. This was followed by an artillery duel, which included the cannon of English ships in the Firth of Forth (the estuary of the River Forth). The Scots now began to crumble under a deluge of artillery, arquebus fire, and arrows. When they routed, the English charged and inflicted up to 6,000 dead on the Scots, losing 500 men themselves.

Despite their resounding defeat, the Scots still refused the marriage, smuggling Queen Mary out of Scotland to France.

1297

WILLIAM WALLACE: SCOURGE OF THE ENGLISH

When King Edward I of England made himself overlord of Scotland in 1290, it provoked rebellions against him. In 1297, the leadership of Sir William Wallace led to a collapse of English power in Scotland, only Dundee Castle holding out. With the king fighting in France, the task of relieving it fell to the Earl of Surrey, who marched 7,000 troops via Stirling Castle.

Wallace and his co-commander Sir William Moray, with 6,000 soldiers, moved to intercept the English at the narrow bridge over the Forth at Stirling (the main crossing point into northern Scotland). Wallace deployed his army on high ground on the northern side of the river, the English attacking him across the bridge with a vanguard of cavalry.

Once around 2,000 cavalry were across the bridge, Wallace's *schiltrons* (formations of spearmen) attacked and pushed the English back. The cavalry was now trapped between the Scots and their own troops, who were still trying to pass over the bridge. A third of the English Army had been destroyed, whereupon Surrey ordered the bridge to be demolished, leaving any survivors on the far bank to their fate. English losses were over 5,000 in a battle that elevated Wallace to become a national hero.

490 BCE

TRIUMPH OF THE HOPLITES AT MARATHON

The first clash of arms between East and West took place on this day, on the Plain of Marathon, northeast of Athens.

The Persian King of Kings Darius the Great invaded Greece in 490 BCE, the Persian commanders Artaphernes and Datis and 26,000 troops mustering on the Plain of Marathon prior to their advance on Athens. Facing them were 9,000 Athenian and 1,000 Plataean hoplites—infantry wearing bronze breastplates, helmets, and greaves, carrying a round shield and armed with a sword and a long spear.

The Athenian general Miltiades weakened his center and strengthened his wings to extend his battle line to match that of the Persians. He then ordered his center to charge, the hoplites covering 1.25 miles (2 km) at speed to smash the Persian center. The Persian wings gave way almost immediately, the survivors fleeing back to their ships, allowing the hoplites to wheel inward to strike the rear of the Persian center. The rout was complete, the Persians suffering more than 6,000 casualties to the Greeks' 192.

The Battle of Marathon later became a powerful symbol of the triumph of Western freedom over Eastern tyranny, which allowed Greek culture and learning to flourish in the decades afterward.

▼ A painting by Georges Antoine Rochegrosse shows the Athenian and Plataean victory over the Persians at the Battle of Marathon.

1759

THE BATTLE THAT GAVE BRITAIN CANADA

To conquer Canada, the British had to capture the town and fortress of Quebec, the task of doing so being given to General James Wolfe. On this day, he and 3,800 troops were on the Plains of Abraham, southwest of the town.

Wolfe deployed his men two ranks deep to face 4,500 French soldiers commanded by the Marquis de Montcalm, the latter ordering his men to assault the British. Both he and Wolfe were shot down, but the British troops held their fire until they French were 10 yards (9 m) away, then fired their muskets. Some 1,400 French soldiers fell in 15 minutes; the rest fled back to Quebec. The Battle of Quebec would lead to the British conquest of Canada a year later.

ALSO ON THIS DAY

533

The Vandal Kingdom in Africa collapses after the Byzantine general Belisarius defeats the Vandal army of King Gelimer at the Battle of Ad Decimum, near Carthage in modern-day Tunisia.

1862

UNION VICTORY OVER LEE AT SOUTH MOUNTAIN

Robert E. Lee led his Army of Northern Virginia on an invasion of Maryland in September 1862.

During the American Civil War, following his success at Second Manassas, the Confederate General Robert E. Lee led his Army of Northern Virginia on an invasion of Maryland in September 1862. He divided his army into two, sending troops into western Maryland and others to take Harpers Ferry, West Virginia. But his plans fell into the hands of the Union commander, General George B. McClellan, who wasted no time in sending six corps (28,000 men) to destroy the 18,000 Confederates defending three passes on South Mountain, Maryland.

The Battle of South Mountain resulted in heavy Confederate casualties—2,685 killed, wounded, or missing—and the loss of the passes. But their dogged resistance allowed Lee to reunite his army, and set the stage for the Battle of Antietam on September 17.

SEPTEMBER 15

1894

JAPANESE VICTORY AT PYONGYANG

The First Sino-Japanese War (1894–5) was fought over control of Korea, and one of the major land engagements of the conflict took place on September 15.

The Japanese 1st Army, commanded by Prince Yamagata Aritomo, attacked Pyongyang during the morning, the 20,000 troops meeting stiff resistance from the 13,000 defenders of China's Beiyang Army (many of whom were armed with modern Western weapons). However, the Japanese captured a fortress to the north of the city, from where they directed artillery fire into Pyongyang. The garrison surrendered later that day, heavy rainfall and the fall of darkness allowing many to escape. Nevertheless, the defense of Pyongyang cost the Chinese 2,000 dead to only 650 Japanese casualties.

▼ China is defeated by Japan's more modern forces during the first Sino-Japanese War.

1776

GEORGE WASHINGTON'S FIRST TASTE OF BATTLEFIELD SUCCESS

Following the British seizure of Manhattan Island on September 15, 1776, during the American Revolutionary War, Continental troops were pushed north in disarray. General George Washington arrived at Harlem Heights, on the northern end of Manhattan, to take command.

On the morning of the 16th, he sent a detachment of rangers under the command of Captain Thomas Knowlton to scout the British positions, which prompted the British troops to engage the rangers in a firefight, pushing them back. Washington then dispatched a second, larger force to attack the British right flank. A short but intense exchange of musketry followed, which forced the British to retreat. The battle cost the British 14 killed and 157 wounded, the Americans 30 killed and 100 wounded. The Battle of Harlem Heights was a minor affair but was the first success for the commander of the Continental Army, George Washington.

1862

BLOODY STALEMATE AT ANTIETAM

In one of the bloodiest battles of the American Civil War, the armies of Confederate general Robert E. Lee and Union general George B. McClellan fought each other along the Antietam Creek, near Sharpsburg, Maryland.

The Union I and XII Corps fought "Stonewall" Jackson's brigades through Miller's Cornfield, at the Hagerstown Turnpike and West Woods. Later in the day the Union II Corps broke through the Confederate center at the Sunken Road, but failed to exploit the gain. Then the Union IX Corps surged across the bridge over Antietam Creek to buckle the Rebel right, but was pushed back by the division of General A. P. Hill arriving from Harpers Ferry. At the end of the day, of the 132,000 troops involved, 22,717 were casualties. It was the bloodiest single day in American history.

It was one of the bloodiest battles of the American Civil War.

CONSTANTINE BECOMES SOLE EMPEROR Valerius Licinianus was executed after a battle with Roman emperor Constantine the Great in Chrysopolis (now part of Istanbul, Turkey).

SEPTEMBER 19
1863

THE START OF THE BATTLE OF CHICKAMAUGA The Braxton Bragg's Confederates defeated William Rosecrans' Union troops in Georgia during the American Civil War.

THE FRENCH REVOLUTION IS SAVED The Prussian advance on Paris to restore the monarchy was stopped by an army of citizens. The battle took place in Valmy, France.

THE WAR OF THE AUSTRIAN SUCCESSION REACHES INDIA French forces compelled the surrender of the British garrison of Madras on India's Carnatic coast.

THE SWORD BROTHERS ARE DEFEATED The Sword Brothers, a Catholic military order based in Livonia on the Baltic, were defeated at Saule by a pagan Lithuanian army.

INDIAN DEFEAT British general Arthur Wellesley and his troops used an unmarked ford over the Kaitna River in Assaye, India, to outflank an army of the Maratha Empire.

ROYALIST TROOPS DEFEATED During the English Civil War, Royalist troops were defeated by Parliamentary forces at the Battle of Rowton Heath.

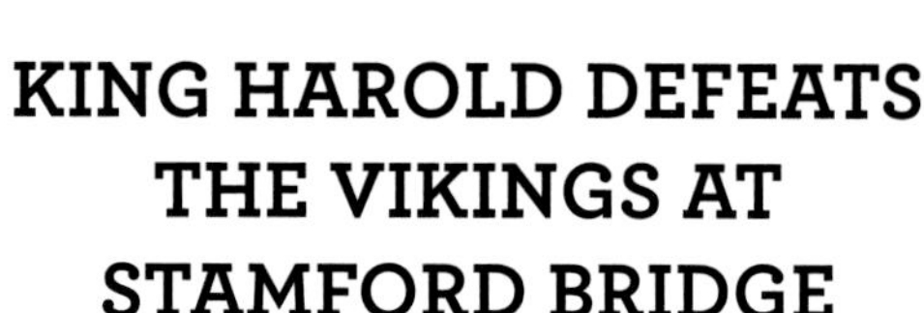

KING HAROLD DEFEATS THE VIKINGS AT STAMFORD BRIDGE

Following the death of King Edward the Confessor of England in January 1066, Harold Godwinson was proclaimed king. But there were other claimants who were prepared to back up their claims with force. One was King Harold Hardrada of Norway, who sailed with 11,000 Vikings in 300 ships and seized York.

Harold immediately marched from London to York, covering 185 miles (296 km) in four days. He and his 15,000 troops attacked the Vikings and broke their shield wall on September 25 at the village of Stamford Bridge just outside York, killing Hardrada and 6,000 of his Vikings (Harold lost 5,000 men). Only 24 longboats returned to Norway.

Harold Godwinson was proclaimed king. But there were other claimants who were prepared to back up their claims with force.

SLAUGHTER AT POLYGON WOOD

On September 26, 1917, during World War I, British and Commonwealth forces attacked Polygon Wood in the Ypres Salient on the Western Front.

The "wood" had been fought over since 1914 and all the trees had been destroyed by shellfire, to be replaced by German concrete strongpoints and barbed wire. Seven divisions took part in the assault, including the 4th and 5th Australian Divisions. By this stage of the war, aircraft were playing a significant part in offensives, and during the assault spotter aircraft were directing British artillery fire to support the infantry.

The Australian troops captured the "Butte," an observation post in the center of the wood, by the end of the day. Fighting would continue until October 3, the Australians repulsing all German attacks. Capturing the wood cost the Allies more than 20,000 casualties.

▼ Gunner Harold Triggs awaits the order to fire an eight-inch gun at Birr Cross Roads, two days before the main attack on Polygon Wood, in Ypres, Belgium.

1810

WELLINGTON OUTFOXES MARSHAL MASSÉNA IN PORTUGAL

When Marshal Masséna and 80,000 French troops crushed the Spanish Army to march into Portugal in the summer of 1810 during the Napoleonic Wars, the Duke of Wellington withdrew to the heights of Bussaco, 125 miles (200 km) northeast of Lisbon. There he intended to block the French with 25,000 British and 25,000 Portuguese troops.

At the Battle of Bussaco fought on this day, Wellington checked Masséna's 60,000 troops, at a cost of 1,200 allied soldiers (the French lost 4,600), but continued his retreat behind the Torres Vedras, a series of fortified lines across the Lisbon Peninsula. Masséna pursued but found the defensive lines too formidable; he was forced to withdraw back into Spain in the spring of 1811.

ALSO ON THIS DAY

1331

At the Battle of Plowce, Poland, a Polish army defeats a force of Teutonic Knights. Both sides suffer heavy casualties and the knights flee unpursued.

1652

BRITISH VICTORY AT KENTISH KNOCK

The Dutch Admiral Tromp was determined to bring the English fleet to battle.

Kentish Knock, a sandbank in the Thames Estuary, lends its name to a sea battle between the English and Dutch that took place during the Anglo-Dutch War.

The Dutch admiral Tromp was determined to bring the English fleet to battle, aiming to clear it from the Straits of Dover to safeguard the English Channel for Dutch commerce. Sailing with a fleet of 62 warships, he encountered the English fleet under General-at-Sea Robert Blake near Kentish Knock. The Dutch fleet formed into three squadrons. English gunnery proved superior to the Dutch and many of Tromp's ships were badly damaged, though only two were lost. The Dutch withdrew, having been thoroughly outgunned during the encounter.

480 BCE

PERSIAN DISASTER IN THE STRAIT OF SALAMIS

The Persian invasion of Greece was initially a disaster for the Greeks on land, and at sea Xerxes' fleet of 600 galleys contained the 366 Greek triremes (ships with three banks of oars) in the Saronic Gulf. But the Greek commander Themistocles, according to legend, lured the Persian fleet into the confined waters of the Strait of Salamis by means of a misleading message, thus seriously restricting the Persians' maneuverability.

In the ensuing Battle of Salamis, the Greek triremes commanded by the Spartan Eurybiades employed ramming and boarding tactics to sink more than 200 (some accounts report 300) Persian vessels for the loss of 40 of their own.

At Salamis, the first decisive battle in history, the Persian fleet was driven from the shores of Europe.

The Persian invasion of Greece was initially a disaster for the Greeks on land.

489

DECISIVE VICTORY FOR THE OSTROGOTHS IN ITALY

Theodoric the Great (455–526) was the Ostrogoth king who led his people from the Danube regions of the Roman Empire to conquer Italy, being encouraged to do so by Emperor Zeno of the Eastern Roman Empire, who wished to be rid of the Ostrogoths himself.

Theodoric decisively defeated Odoacer, King of Italy, at the Battle of Verona on September 30. Odoacer beat a hasty retreat to his capital at Ravenna, leaving the Otstrogoths in control of northern Italy. Theodoric then laid siege to Ravenna, but the town was protected by marshes on the landward side and had access to the sea, which made it a hard nut to crack. The siege would last for two and a half years.

ALSO ON THIS DAY

1744

A Franco-Spanish army defeats the Sardinians at the Battle of Cuneo, Piedmont, during the War of the Austrian Succession.

CHAPTER
10
October

331 BCE

THE BATTLE THAT WON ALEXANDER THE GREAT HALF THE WORLD

Alexander the Great (356–323 BCE), the young king of Macedonia, invaded the Persian Empire in 334 BCE, crossing the Hellespont (a strait in what is now Turkey), never to return.

Alexander defeated the Persian King of Kings Darius III at Issus in 333 BCE, but two years later Darius led 200,000 soldiers to the plain of Gaugamela, near the ancient city of Nineveh in Upper Mesopotamia. Alexander offered battle with 40,000 foot soldiers and 7,000 horsemen.

The battle opened with Alexander leading an assault with most of his cavalry on the right wing, while his infantry attacked the Persian center. The Persians pressed the Greek foot soldiers, threatening to overwhelm Alexander's center. But then, bizarrely, a mass of Persian cavalry became embroiled in the fighting on Alexander's right flank, leaving the Persian infantry in the center exposed. Alexander himself then led his personal bodyguard, the Companions, against the Persian flank and rear, which relieved the pressure on the Greek center.

At that moment, Darius fled and handed the battle to Alexander, even though his army was still intact and fighting well. The flight of their demigod spread panic throughout the Persian ranks, masses fleeing the battlefield, only to be cut down by pursuing Greeks. Persian losses are estimated at anything between 40,000 and 90,000, with Greek losses at 500. The victory made Alexander master of Asia.

▲ An oil painting by Brueghel the Elder, depicting the Battle of Gaugamela.

1263

THE LAST VIKING INVASION OF SCOTLAND

In the 13th century, the Scottish isles of Bute and Cumbrae, just across from the Scottish-controlled town of Largs on the country's west coast, were Viking lands. These Norsemen were from Norway, which was under the rule of King Haakon IV, while Scotland was ruled by Alexander II. The two fought for control of the west coast islands, Alexander raiding the islands to kill the occupiers. In response, Haakon assembled a fleet of 120 longships to sail down the west coast, only for his fleet to be scattered by a violent storm on October 1, 1263.

Haakon managed to get ashore at Largs with a few hundred men, where they were attacked on October 2 in the Battle of Largs by a Scottish force of several hundred. The battle was a desultory affair that petered out when Haakon and his men reboarded their ships, but it was subsequently portrayed as a great Scottish victory.

In the 13th century, the Scottish isles of Bute and Cumbrae were Viking lands.

1569

CATHOLIC VICTORY OVER THE HUGUENOTS Duc d'Anjou led the Catholics to victory over the Huguenots at Moncontour, France, during the French Wars of Religion.

1636

DEFEAT FOR THE IMPERIAL ARMY During the Thirty Years' War, 20,000 Protestant troops defeated an Imperial army of 30,000 men at Wittstock, northwest of Berlin.

1813

THAMES RIVER BATTLE The American victory over the British and their Indian allies on the Thames River in Ontario, Canada, cemented its control over the Old Northwest.

1973

ATTACK ON ISRAEL Syrian and Egyptian forces attacked Israel and began the Yom Kippur War. Egyptian forces crossed the Suez Canal and Syrian troops made gains on the Golan Heights.

1777

BRITISH ARE REPULSED General Burgoyne's British force was repulsed by Continental troops led by General Benedict Arnold in the Second Battle of Saratoga, in New York state.

1862

THE HEARTLAND CAMPAIGN ENDS AT PERRYVILLE Despite victory, Confederate Bragg was forced to retreat from Kentucky after the final battle of his Heartland campaign.

1708

DECISIVE BATTLE IN THE GREAT NORTHERN WAR Peter the Great's Russian army defeated General Lewenhaupt's Swedish army at Lesnaya in Poland (now Lyasnaya).

732

CHARLES MARTEL HALTS MUSLIM EXPANSION IN CHRISTIAN EUROPE

The victory of the Frankish leader Charles Martel over a Muslim army in 732 ended Islamic expansion into western Europe.

Under the leadership of their governor, Abd ar-Rahman, the Muslims of Spain captured Nîmes and conquered the Frankish province of Septimania. In 732, the governor's large army (perhaps 70,000 in total) defeated Duke Eudo's Aquitainians at the Battle of Bordeaux, and then marched north toward the Loire River. Eudo appealed to Martel, who led an army to intercept the Muslim force. The two armies clashed near Poitiers on this day.

Charles, with 30,000 men, had chosen wooded terrain to negate the mobility of the Muslim horsemen, and dismounted all his men to form a solid shield wall. The Berber and Arab cavalry charged the Franks, whose spears and shields held off the horsemen. However, as evening approached, the exhausted Frankish soldiers began to waver.

With the Franks on the verge of defeat, word spread among the Muslim horsemen that the enemy was raiding their camp, prompting many to disengage. Charles ordered an immediate assault, during which Abd ar-Rahman was killed. The Muslim leader's army then fell apart, up to 10,000 of his men being killed.

1797

THE ROYAL NAVY VICTORIOUS AT CAMPERDOWN

During the French Revolutionary War, the Dutch Republic was overrun by France, becoming an ally of Paris and enemy of Britain. At the Battle of Camperdown, fought this day, a Dutch fleet of 25 ships, commanded by Admiral Jan Willem de Winter, put out from Texel, to be intercepted by 24 British warships commanded by Admiral Adam Duncan.

The British attacked in two columns at speed to prevent the Dutch from reaching the protection of shallow waters near the coast. In a brisk battle, 11 Dutch ships were captured without the loss of a single British ship (though many were too damaged to undertake a pursuit afterward).

ALSO ON THIS DAY

1643

During the English Civil War, a Parliamentary army of infantry and cavalry defeats a Royalist cavalry force at the Battle of Winceby, Lincolnshire.

1917

NEW ZEALAND'S BLACKEST DAY

The 1917 Battle of Passchendaele in World War I has come to symbolize the futile waste of life which characterized that conflict. An incident during the battle, which lasted from July 31 until November 10, was the attack by New Zealand forces on Bellevue Spur, the second of the small rises leading to the Passchendaele Ridge, on October 12.

The New Zealand Division's attack began in the morning, the ground having been turned into a quagmire by the torrential rain (which had rendered the preliminary artillery barrage ineffective). Exposed to German machine-gun fire and unable to penetrate dense barbed wire, the New Zealanders suffered heavy losses, 957 killed on this day alone. The attack petered out, and plans for a fresh assault in the afternoon were canceled. This was just one incident in an offensive that cost hundreds of thousands of lives.

▼ New Zealand engineers rest in a large shell hole at Spree Farm, Passchendaele, in 1917, during World War I.

1644

SWEDISH NAVAL VICTORY OVER THE DANES AT FEHMARN

The Thirty Years' War was a disaster for Germany, up to a third of its population dying in a conflict that destroyed hundreds of villages. But for some nations, such as Sweden, it presented an opportunity to extend their power and territory.

The rise of Sweden brought it into conflict with Denmark over the control of the Baltic Sea, which resulted in several naval battles between the two states. In general, Danish ships and their crews were superior to their Swedish adversaries, but at the Battle of Fehmarn the Swedes were reinforced by a fleet of 21 Dutch vessels.

The Dutch–Swedish fleet of 37 ships engaged the Danish fleet northwest of the island of Fehmarn off the German Baltic coast, dividing into five squadrons, while the Danish fleet divided into two. The two sides began exchanging broadsides at around 10:00 hours, the smaller Danish vessels retiring, to be pursued by the Dutch ships. Two Swedish ships boarded the Danish flagship *Patientia*, while another Danish vessel, the *Lindormen*, exploded when attacked by a Swedish fireship. In all, the Danes lost 12 ships to one Swedish vessel sunk. The Battle of Fehmarn gave Sweden dominance over the Baltic Sea.

1066

WILLIAM THE CONQUEROR WINS THE CROWN OF ENGLAND

When William of Normandy landed on the Sussex coast in late September 1066, King Harold of England, fresh from his victory at Stamford Bridge, rushed south to block William's advance on London. He and his 7,000 Saxons deployed on Senlac Hill, 8 miles (13 km) north of Hastings. On October 14, William and his army of 7,000 soldiers gave battle to the Saxons.

The first charge of Norman knights was repulsed by the Saxons, who then charged down the hill, to be cut down by the Normans. Harold reorganized his battle line, and his men stood firm under a storm of arrows and more cavalry charges. But as evening approached, William feigned a withdrawal of his cavalry, prompting the Saxons to rush down the hill to complete their victory. William's horsemen wheeled around and slaughtered the Saxons. The last remaining Saxon warriors, Harold's bodyguard, fell defending their king, who was mortally wounded when, according to legend, an arrow penetrated his eye. Both sides had lost around a quarter of their armies, but crucially, William's victory allowed him to march on London.

William was crowned King of England on Christmas Day 1066, making the Battle of Hastings one of the most decisive battles ever fought on English soil.

1793

KEEPING THE FRENCH REVOLUTION ALIVE

Revolutionary France's offer of aid to those wishing to promote revolt in their own countries led the monarchical states of Britain, Holland, Spain, Austria, Prussia, and Russia to form the First Coalition against France in 1792. After early Allied victories, the French Constitutional Convention formed citizen armies by mass mobilization and went on the offensive.

The French relieved the port of Dunkirk in September 1793 and then turned their attention to Mauberge near the Belgian border, which was besieged by Allied forces commanded by the Prince of Saxe-Coburg. If it had fallen, the last remaining fortress barring the way to Pairs would have been captured by the enemies of France. French general Jean-Baptiste Jourdan was therefore dispatched with an army of 50,000 conscripts to attack the chiefly Austrian army of some 26,000 troops besieging the fortress at Maubeuge (on the plateau of Wattignies).

The Battle of Wattignies, which began on October 15, started badly for the French, their poorly organized troops being beaten back by the Austrian professionals. However, during the evening Jourdan shifted 8,000 men from his left flank to his right, near Wattignies village itself. This maneuver overlapped the Austrian right, so that on the morning of the 16th, Saxe-Coburg's entire battle line was rolled up. He was forced to retreat and therefore abandon the siege. The Allied advance on Paris had been stopped in its tracks.

▲ The Battle of Wattignies during the War of the First Coalition.

1973

EGYPTIANS AND ISRAELIS SLUG IT OUT AT "CHINESE FARM"

The narrow Israeli corridor was threatened by the Egyptian possession of "Chinese Farm," a settlement in the Sinai Desert.

During the 1973 Yom Kippur War, Israeli forces mounted a counterattack against Egyptian positions in the Sinai Peninsula. The narrow Israeli corridor was threatened by the Egyptian possession of "Chinese Farm," a former agricultural settlement in the Sinai Desert.

The task of capturing the farm was given to a battalion of the Israeli 35th Paratroop Brigade, which attacked on October 16, only to be thrown back by dogged Egyptian resistance. The battle went on into the night and all the next day, the lightly armed paratroopers coming under artillery and anti-tank fire. But they held firm in the face of overwhelming odds, the battalion losing 40 killed and 100 wounded.

The paratroopers kept the Egyptians occupied long enough to allow other units to bypass the farm and head for the Suez Canal.

▼ Soldiers take a route through the Sinai Desert.

1448

OTTOMAN TRIUMPH AT KOSOVO

In response to the growing Ottoman threat, the Hungarian leader János Hunyadi led an army of 24,000 troops into Serbia, reaching as far as Kosovo. Sultan Murad II hurried north with a well-trained army of 40,000 men to confront Hunyadi. The resulting Battle of Kosovo began on October 17.

Hunyadi placed his pikemen and handgunners in the center, his cavalry on both flanks. The battle on the first day was a stalemate, both sides incurring substantial losses. On the 18th, however, the Hungarian cavalry were bested by the Ottoman mailed horsemen, forcing Hunyadi to withdraw his army. The two-day battle cost the Ottomans a third of their army, while almost half of the Hungarians lay dead. The Balkans had been cleared and Murad was free to threaten Constantinople.

In response to the growing Ottoman threat, the Hungarian leader János Hunyadi led an army of 24,000 troops into Serbia.

1016

VIKING VICTORY IN ESSEX

Afterward, Cnut and Edmund made peace.

Cnut the Great (995–1035) was a legendary Viking leader. He landed in England with his father, King Sweyn of Denmark, in 1013 and became king on Sweyn's death a year later. But his desire for the English crown brought him into conflict with Edmund II "Ironside" of Wessex.

The two fought each other at the Battle of Assandun in Essex (present-day Ashingdon, or possibly Ashdon), on October 18. Edmund and his Saxons were on the verge of victory when his brother-in-law, Edric, deserted to the Danes with his men. The Saxon army, weakened and demoralized, could not resist the charge of Cnut's Vikings, and was decisively defeated. Afterward, Cnut and Edmund made peace, the former winning all of England aside from Wessex, which he inherited after Edmund's death later in 1016.

AMERICA WINS ITS FREEDOM AT YORKTOWN

In October 1781, during the American Revolutionary War, the main British army, commanded by General Lord Cornwallis, was under siege in the Virginian town of Yorktown. His 6,000 soldiers faced over 16,000 American and French troops under the commands of George Washington and the Comte de Rochambeau, respectively. French ships were also enforcing a naval blockade of Yorktown.

The siege lines had been established by October 6, and artillery began pounding British positions on the 9th. When British sorties on October 16 failed to prevent the closer emplacement of the siege artillery, Cornwallis lost all hope and accepted surrender terms.

At 14:00 hours on this day, British troops marched out of Yorktown and laid down their arms. Across the York River, Colonel Banastre Tarleton surrendered the garrison of Gloucester. The surrender at Yorktown ended the fighting in America. The colonists had won their freedom.

▼ The British surrender at Yorktown.

DESTRUCTION OF THE TURKISH FLEET AT NAVARINO

The Greek War of Independence fought against the Ottoman Turks began in 1821, and after some early successes, the tide turned against the insurgents. The Turks responded to the revolt with brutality, their troops massacring the Christians on Crete, for example. In 1827, Athens itself fell and the flame of Greek resistance was on the verge of being snuffed out.

Alarmed by Turkish atrocities, Britain, France, and Russia demanded Ottoman forces to withdraw from Greece. When this was ignored, they dispatched a combined fleet of 24 ships under the command of Admiral Sir Edward Codrington, which entered the harbor of Navarino, in the southwestern Peloponnese, on October 20. At anchor was the entire Egyptian fleet of Mehemet (Mohammed) Ali, plus a number of Ottoman vessels.

With superior firepower and well-trained crews, the Allied fleet sank more than 50 Egyptian–Ottoman vessels and ran others aground. French troops would drive out the Egyptian forces from Greece.

Navarino was the last pitched battle between wooden sailing ships.

▼ Ships in combat during the Battle of Navarino, part of the Greek War of Independence.

1805

"ENGAGE THE ENEMY MORE CLOSELY"— NELSON'S MASTERPIECE

Sea battles in the age of wooden fighting ships were often blunt affairs. The vessels were essentially of only one type: armed with crude, inaccurate cannon, which to be of any use had to be mounted in broadsides. As a result, fleets adopted a "line ahead" formation to engage their opponents. Occasionally, talented admirals would adapt their tactics to suit their ships. Admiral Horatio Nelson did just that.

Thus, when on October 19, 33 French and Spanish ships slipped out of Cádiz to make a dash for the Strait of Gibraltar, they were attacked by Nelson's fleet of 27 warships, deployed in two columns, 10 miles (16 km) off Cape Trafalgar. Nelson knew his crews and their captains were better trained than their opponents.

The British ships pierced the enemy line in a hard-fought action, 18 French and Spanish ships surrendering and the remainder fleeing. Only 11 made it back to Cádiz. No British ship was lost, though Nelson was mortally wounded and 1,500 British sailors were killed or wounded. French and Spanish killed, wounded, and captured numbered 14,000.

The Battle of Trafalgar was one of the most decisive naval battles in military history, one which made the Royal Navy mistress of the seas for over a century.

1777

AMERICAN VICTORY AGAINST THE ODDS AT RED BANK

During the American Revolutionary War, Fort Mercer on the Delaware River was the scene of a surprising victory. During this conflict the British used troops from Hesse in Germany, and it was 1,200 German soldiers, under the command of Colonel Carl von Donop, that attacked the fort, supported by six British warships on the river. Defending the fort were 400 militia, commanded by Colonel Christopher Greene, supported by a small flotilla of boats on the Delaware.

The two-pronged attack on the fort was a disaster.

The two-pronged attack on the fort was a disaster, the defenders shooting down more than 80 Hessians and wounding 228 more. Unable to breach the fort's defenses, the attackers withdrew, leaving a mortally wounded von Donop behind. And on the Delaware one of the British ships, which had run aground on the 22nd, caught fire and exploded the next day.

42 BCE

AVENGING CAESAR'S MURDER AT THE BATTLE OF PHILIPPI

Following the assassination of Julius Caesar, a large Republican army mustered in Macedonia under the leadership of Marcus Brutus and Gaius Cassius, two of the leaders in the plot to kill Caesar. The triumvirs Mark Antony and Octavian marched with an army to Greece to intercept them. The two forces clashed at Philippi in Macedonia on October 3, 42 BCE, the first battle proving inconclusive, though Cassius committed suicide when his legions were routed on the left wing by Mark Antony.

After a three-week break, the decisive second Battle of Philippi took place on the 23rd, the legions of Octavian pushing back Brutus' legionaries, routing his army. Rather than be captured, Brutus committed suicide.

A large Republican army mustered in Macedonia under the leadership of Marcus Brutus and Gaius Cassius, two leaders of the plot to kill Caesar.

1918

COLLAPSE OF AUSTRIAN RESISTANCE IN ITALY

The bloodletting in northern Italy in World War I came to a head at the Battle of Vittorio Veneto.

The Italian supreme commander, General Armando Diaz, massed 57 divisions and 7,700 artillery pieces against the Austrians' 52 divisions and 6,000 artillery pieces. When the attack began, the Italian 4th Army immediately ran into difficulties, being counterattacked by Austrian troops. The 8th, 10th, and 12th Italian armies were likewise contained just beyond the Piave River, though the 10th was able to establish a bridgehead that Diaz was to exploit to create a break in the Austrian line.

Suddenly, Austrian resistance began to collapse (many units had poor morale), the Italian 8th Army capturing Vittorio Veneto on October 30. Austrian divisions began to flee from the province of Trentino to the Adriatic, Italian cavalry and armored cars rounding up thousands of prisoners. Faced with certain defeat, the Austrians signed a truce at Villa Giusti, near Padua, on November 3, by which date the Italians had captured 500,000 prisoners.

During the battle the Italians had suffered 38,000 casualties, but the war had cost Italy 650,000 dead and almost one million wounded. The Austro-Hungarians had suffered 400,000 dead and 1.2 million wounded on the Italian Front.

1415

TRIUMPH OF THE LONGBOW AT AGINCOURT

During the Hundred Years' War, King Henry V of England was retreating before a large French army of 10,000 men-at-arms and up to 20,000 supporting foot soldiers under Constable Charles d'Albret and Marshal Jean Boucicaut.

Henry and his army of 1,000 men-at-arms and 5,000 archers were brought to heel at the village of Agincourt (now Azincourt), south of Calais. He was forced to deploy his army in a narrow gap between two woods, obliging the French to assault his soldiers frontally and thus negating somewhat their superior numbers.

The first French assault, despite heavy casualties from arrows, reached the English line. A second French assault was beaten back with arrows, axes and swords, leaving the duke dead on the field. An assault on the English camp by French camp followers led Henry to believe he was surrounded and order his French prisoners to be killed.

A third French assault never materialized, the ground in front of the French soldiers being already heaped with 6,000 of their dead comrades. English losses were around 1,600. In the space of a few hours Henry V had decimated the French nobility and secured one of the great victories in history.

▼ The French and English battle at Agincourt, France, with archers positioned in front and cavalry massed behind them.

1942

MAULING OF U.S. CARRIERS AT SANTA CRUZ

The fight for the Solomon Islands, in the Pacific Theater of World War II, lasted longer than any other Allied campaign of the Pacific War, from August 1942 to March 1944. It was fought on land and at sea.

The naval battle of Santa Cruz was one action during the fight for the Solomons. It was the first action in the Guadalcanal campaign for the new supreme Allied commander in the South Pacific, Admiral William Halsey, who sent his aircraft carriers against the Japanese fleet to the east of the Solomons. His carrier aircraft achieved some success, hitting two enemy carriers and a cruiser, and shooting down 100 Japanese aircraft. But 74 U.S. aircraft were lost, the carrier *Hornet* was sunk, and the carrier *Enterprise* damaged, which meant there was not one U.S. carrier in operation in the entire Pacific.

The fight for the Solomon Islands lasted longer than any other Allied campaign of the Pacific War.

1644

A LOST OPPORTUNITY FOR PARLIAMENT AT NEWBURY

In 1644, during the English Civil War, Parliament had won a great victory at Marston Moor, but King Charles had forced the surrender of the Earl of Essex's army at Lostwithiel, Cornwall. The king then marched east to threaten London, arriving near the town of Newbury with 9,000 troops. Parliament dispatched the Earl of Manchester to stop him. By October 26, Manchester had 17,500 troops mustered near Newbury. The battle took place the following day.

King Charles had forced the surrender of the Earl of Essex's army at Lostwithiel, Cornwall.

The Roundheads attempted a pincer attack on the strong Royalist position. But William Waller's attack from the west was stopped in its tracks, and in the east the Earl of Manchester attacked half-heartedly. The king was still trapped between two enemy armies, but escaped during the evening. The drawn battle had been a lost opportunity for the Parliament to end the Civil War by capturing the king himself.

THE BATTLE THAT CONVERTED THE ROMAN EMPIRE TO CHRISTIANITY

In 312, the army of Marcus Aurelius Valerius Maxentius, 100,000-strong, gave battle to the Roman Emperor Constantine the Great at the Milvian Bridge, near Rome. The imperial soldiers were carrying Christian symbols on their shields, for Constantine had seen a vision of a burning cross on the night before the battle. Convinced the Christian God was on his side, he ordered his men to paint their shields with the Chi-Rho (X-P) symbol.

On October 28, Maxentius' troops crossed the Tiber on a pontoon bridge on the site of the demolished Milvian Bridge. His inexperienced troops were outflanked by Constantine's cavalry and routed, fleeing back across the bridge, which collapsed. Thousands drowned or were cut down by their pursuers.

Attributing his victory to the intervention of God, a year after the Battle of Milvian Bridge, Constantine made Christianity the official religion of the empire.

Constantine made Christianity the official religion of the empire.

◀ The Battle of Milvian Bridge saw the death of Maxentius.

1762

LAST PRUSSIAN VICTORY IN THE SEVEN YEARS' WAR

The Seven Years' War (1756–63) exhausted the participants, and by 1762 only Prussia and Austria were still fighting. With neither wanting a large-scale battle, the Battle of Freiberg, southwest of Dresden, was a minor affair, notable only for being the last major engagement of the war in Europe.

Prince Henry Ludwig and General Friedrich von Seydlitz's Prussian forces made a three-pronged attack on the Austrian Army; despite dogged resistance, Prince Stolberg's Austrian force was broken after three hours of fighting. After suffering 3,000 dead and wounded out of their total of 30,000, the Austrians retreated. Of the 22,000 Prussian troops, 1,500 were killed or wounded.

ALSO ON THIS DAY

1658

At the Battle of the Sound, a Dutch fleet of 45 ships defeats a Swedish force of 43 ships just north of the Danish capital of Copenhagen, thus ending the Swedish blockade of the city.

1805

MARSHAL MASSÉNA SECURES NAPOLEON'S SOUTHERN FLANK

In late September 1805, when Napoleon marched his Grande Armée into central Europe to deal with the Austrians and Russians, in order to achieve success he had to keep the Austrian armies of Archdukes John and Charles (in Tyrol and northern Italy, respectively) out of the Danube River area. To this end, on Otober 30 Marshal Masséna, commanding 50,000 troops, fought Archduke Charles, with a similar number of soldiers, at the Battle of Caldiero, 9 miles (15 km) east of Verona, Italy.

Archduke Charles opened the battle, assaulting both French flanks and achieving some success before the French rallied and held the attacks. In the center, the fight for Caldiero lasted all day, the French eventually taking the village after hand-to-hand combat.

For the loss of 3,200 killed and wounded, Masséna had defeated Archduke Charles and prevented him marching north of the Tyrol, the Austrians suffering 9,000 killed, wounded, and captured.

CHARGE OF THE AUSTRALIAN LIGHT HORSE AT BEERSHEBA

In October 1917 in the Middle East, during World War I, British and Commonwealth troops were poised to capture Gaza, the gateway to Palestine. The British commander, General Sir Edmund Allenby, decided to focus on the town of Beersheba, on the eastern flank of the Turkish defensive line. While three British divisions attacked the main Turkish defenses on the outskirts of Beersheba, New Zealand and Australian mounted troops would ride to the east to assault the town from the rear.

In the Battle of Beersheba, the New Zealand Mounted Rifles Brigade captured a fortified hill northeast of the town to create an opening to capture Beersheba itself. With light fading, the 4th Australian Light Horse Brigade charged into the town, taking the defenders by surprise. Beersheba and its important wells had been captured. The Turkish 7th Army fell back in disarray.

▼ Turkish lancers west of Beersheba during the Battle of Beersheba.

CHAPTER
11
November

THE NAVAL DEFEAT THAT SHOOK THE BRITISH EMPIRE

When World War I broke out in August 1914, Britain's Royal Navy ruled the waves. In terms of the number of fighting ships, modernity, and the caliber of its crews, it was far ahead of other leading maritime powers. On land, the German Army might have been a formidable force, but at sea the Royal Navy expected to defeat the Imperial German Navy in its first encounter.

When war broke out, the Germans had a small number of ships on the high seas, one group comprising five cruisers under the command of Admiral Count Maximilian von Spee, which sailed from the Orient to arrive off Coronel, Chile, on November 1, where they were engaged in battle by a British squadron commanded by Admiral Sir Christopher Craddock.

At the Battle of Coronel, Craddock had two heavy cruisers (*Good Hope* and *Monmouth*), a light cruiser (*Glasgow*), and an auxiliary cruiser (*Otranto*). In a short engagement, the German ships sank the two heavy cruisers, the other two ships escaping. Craddock himself went down on the *Good Hope* and 1,600 British sailors were killed. No German ships were lost. The defeat at Coronel made headline news around the world and dealt a heavy blow to British morale.

▼ Photograph of the British cruiser *Monmouth*.

1912

OTTOMAN DEFEAT IN THRACE

The beginning of the 20th century saw the decline of the Ottoman Empire, with its outdated army and navy unable to safeguard Turkish possessions in the Balkans, Africa, and the Middle East. The Balkans, Greece, Serbia, Bulgaria, and Montenegro waged a combined war against them in 1912–13, the First Balkan War, resulting in a number of reverses.

One such defeat was the Battle of Lule Burgas, which concluded on November 2. A Bulgarian army of 108,000 men attacked Turkish positions at Lule Burgas, 86 miles (129 km) northwest of Constantinople, defended by 130,000 Ottoman troops. After three days of combat, the Ottomans broke and began to retreat after losing 22,000 killed and wounded. Bulgarian losses were 19,500 killed and wounded.

ALSO ON THIS DAY

1940

The Battle of Elaia-Kalamas begins between Greek and Italian forces in Epirus, Greece, during World War II. The Greeks prove victorious on November 8.

1760

PRUSSIA'S IRON DISCIPLINE AT TORGAU

The Prussian Army of Frederick the Great was noted for its firepower, its ability to march long distances and fight a battle at the end, and its unwavering obedience to orders, even in the face of enemy fire.

When the Austrian field marshal Leopold von Daun established a fortified camp at Torgau on the Elbe River during the Seven Years' War, Frederick marched to give battle, despite being outnumbered 65,000 to 44,000. In a two-pronged attack on November 3, Frederick's infantry marched into the full force of the enemy's cannon and muskets. Of the 6,000 Prussian troops that made the initial assault, only 600 survived. But Frederick kept feeding his infantry into the killing zone, eventually winning the Battle of Torgau but at a cost of a third of his army.

ALSO ON THIS DAY

1812

During Napoleon's retreat from Moscow, the rearguard of the French Army is defeated by Russian forces at the Battle of Vyazma.

1942

MONTY'S MASTERPIECE AT EL ALAMEIN

The Battle of El Alamein in Egypt, which concluded on November 4, was the turning point in the war in North Africa.

The Battle of El Alamein in Egypt was the turning point in the war in North Africa.

When General Bernard Montgomery, commander of the British 8th Army, began the battle on October 23, he had at his disposal 195,000 troops, 1,029 tanks, and 530 aircraft. Field Marshal Erwin Rommel's Panzer Army Africa, by comparison, had only 100,000 troops, 489 tanks, and 340 aircraft. Nevertheless, Axis forces fought well during the first week of the battle, being gradually ground down by superior numbers and lack of fuel and ammunition. Inevitably, the Axis line cracked and then collapsed, British armor pouring through the gaps and hounding Axis forces westward. In seven months, the Axis war effort in North Africa would collapse.

1757

PRUSSIAN TRIUMPH AT ROSSBACH

The Battle of Rossbach, fought on November 5 in Saxony, was a tactical masterpiece by Frederick the Great, who fought a 41,000-strong Franco-Imperialist army with only 22,000 troops.

The Allies, marching in five columns, were deceived by Frederick who moved his army behind Janus Hill, prompting them to believe he was retreating. Meanwhile, the Prussian cavalry commander, Seydlitz, massed his men behind Polsen Hill, timing his charge to perfection in order to rout the Allied cavalry. Frederick's infantry then charged the Allied foot soldiers, causing the French to flee. Seydlitz then charged again, into the Allied flank, causing the entire Allied army to fall to pieces, with the loss of 10,000 men. Prussian casualties were 550.

ALSO ON THIS DAY

1950

British and Australian troops repulse Chinese forces at the Battle of Pakchon, during the Korean War—the route allows United Nations units to withdraw safely.

VIVE LA RÉPUBLIQUE!

Following its victory at the Battle of Valmy in September 1792, the Revolutionary French National Convention in Paris ordered an offensive in Flanders in the fall of the same year. Naturally it chose the victor of Valmy, General Charles Dumouriez, to command the ragtag army of 40,000, which contained many raw volunteers.

The French Army duly marched north and ran into 14,000 Austrian soldiers entrenched at Jemappes, just west of Mons. At the battle of the same name fought on November 6, Dumouriez launched his ill-trained recruits in a frontal charge against the Austrians, routing them. The Austrian commander, Duke Albert of Saxe-Teschen, subsequently resigned his command and the French went on to conquer the Austrian Netherlands.

ALSO ON THIS DAY

1917

The Battle of Passchendaele ends on the Western Front in World War I after three months of futile Allied attacks.

GRANT SEES VICTORY SNATCHED AWAY AT BELMONT

During the American Civil War, Union commander Ulysses S. Grant made plans to capture the Rebel stronghold of Columbus, Kentucky, just across the Mississippi River from Belmont, Missouri, by first capturing the latter.

In November 1861, Belmont was defended by 1,000 Confederate troops; they were attacked on November 7 by the 3,000 men Grant had brought down the river by boat from Cairo, Illinois. General Polk at Columbus sent 2,500 men across the river to assist in the fight against Grant, but the Union troops defeated both them and the 1,000 at Belmont. Polk then sent more men to Belmont, forcing Grant to retire to Cairo.

The Battle of Belmont cost Grant 120 dead and 487 wounded for no result, the Confederates losing 105 dead and 536 wounded or captured.

Union commander Ulysses S. Grant made plans to capture the Rebel stronghold of Columbus, Kentucky.

1620

DEFEAT OF THE WINTER KING

In 1619, Protestant Bohemia gave its throne to Frederick V of the Palatinate, rather than the Catholic Holy Roman Emperor Ferdinand II. As a consequence, a Catholic army under the command of Field Marshal von Tilly was sent to invade Bohemia to destroy Frederick's army and send a clear message that Habsburg rule was not to be challenged.

At the Battle of White Mountain, so named because the two armies clashed on the white chalk mountain outside the city of Prague, Tilly's Catholic force of 25,000 men charged uphill against the demoralized and near-mutinous Protestant forces of Christian of Anhalt (15,000-strong).

The day had dawned misty, covering the Catholic advance, which was also supported by an artillery bombardment. The Protestants, taken by surprise, managed a brief resistance before breaking and fleeing. In a short space of time, a third of Anhalt's army had been killed or captured.

Frederick was nicknamed "the Winter King," referring to the duration of his reign. With his queen (the sister of Charles I of England), he fled Prague, which was occupied and sacked by Tilly's soldiers. The emperor had firmly re-established Catholic rule and the Protestant cause appeared to be lost.

▼ A canvas by Pieter Snayers, depicting the Battle of White Mountain near Prague.

1813

VICTORY FOR ANDREW JACKSON IN THE CREEK WAR

The Creek War of 1813–14 saw American militiamen, commanded by General Andrew Jackson, fight a number of battles against Creek Indians in Georgia and Alabama in response to Creek atrocities, such as the killing of 500 settlers at Fort Mims on the lower Alabama River. In the Battle of Talladega, fought on this day in Alabama, 154 friendly Creeks were besieged by hostile warriors in Fort Henry, near the village of Talladega.

Jackson advanced with 1,200 militia infantry and 800 cavalry and attacked the besiegers, killing 300 warriors in the battle. Due to the retreat of some militia companies, however, 700 warriors were able to escape Jackson's trap.

ALSO ON THIS DAY

1780

A British force attempting to wipe out a camp of enemy militia is defeated at the Battle of Fishdam Ford in South Carolina, during the American Revolutionary War.

1567

HUGUENOT VICTORY AT SAINT-DENIS

In the 16th century, France was racked by religious wars between Catholics and Protestant Huguenots. During the Second War of Religion (1567–8), a Huguenot army, commanded by the Prince de Condé and Gaspard de Coligny, approached Paris, taking up a position at Saint-Denis, immediately north of the city, from where he could interrupt food supplies to the capital.

France was racked by religious wars between Catholics and Protestant Huguenots.

After negotiations failed, King Charles IX sent a royal army, commanded by the Duke of Montmorency, to offer battle to the Protestants. The latter had 1,500 cavalry and 1,200 infantry, the Royalists mustering 16,000 infantry and 3,000 cavalry.

Undeterred by these odds, Coligny charged and broke the Royalist left wing, while Condé attacked and broke the enemy center. Montmorency was mortally wounded, but the Royalist army was too large to be overwhelmed by so small a force, and so the battle ended in a draw at nightfall.

DARING RAID AGAINST TARANTO IN WORLD WAR II

The Italian Navy posed a major threat to the Royal Navy in the Mediterranean in 1940. Possessing 84 surface ships, 67 torpedo boats, and 116 submarines, it had the potential to wreak havoc on British ships transporting men and supplies to North Africa and Malta. The main strength of the Italian Navy was based at Taranto, southern Italy, and so the British decided to attack the base using torpedo-bombers.

The plan, codenamed Judgement, would be the first aerial raid launched from an aircraft carrier against a fleet in a defended harbor. On November 11, the outer harbor contained six battleships, three heavy cruisers, and seven destroyers, while in the inner harbor were four heavy cruisers, two light cruisers, 21 cruisers, and a number of submarines and smaller ships.

The aircraft detailed to attack the ships at Taranto were aged Fairey Swordfish, fabric-covered biplanes with a torpedo slung under the fuselage.

The first wave of Swordfish (12 aircraft) flew from H.M.S. *Illustrious*, 180 miles (290 km) southeast of Taranto, at 20:30 hours on November 10, followed by a second wave of nine aircraft.

After the raid, the battleships *Littorio*, *Caio Duilio*, and *Cavour* were either sunk or beached to prevent them sinking. The heavy cruiser *Trento* was damaged, as were the destroyers *Libeccio* and *Pessagno*; two fleet auxiliaries were also damaged. Two Swordfish were lost during the raid.

▼ The Italian submarine, R.I.N. *Macalle*, in Taranto Harbor.

1942

THE MOST CHAOTIC BATTLE OF WORLD WAR II

The battle for supremacy in the southern Solomon Islands in the Pacific reached a climax in November 1942. Both sides were reinforcing their ground forces on the island of Guadalcanal when a Japanese convoy of transports and 12 destroyers, preceded by the battleships *Hiei* and *Kirishima*, ran into a U.S. Navy force of five cruisers and eight destroyers, commanded by Admiral Daniel Callaghan, in Iron Bottom Bay on the evening of the 12th.

In the furious 30-minute First Naval Battle of Guadalcanal, three U.S. destroyers and two cruisers were sunk and a third cruiser was disabled. Callaghan was killed on the bridge of his flagship, U.S.S. *San Francisco*.

The First Naval Battle of Guadalcanal was a furious battle lasting 30 minutes.

2001

KABUL FALLS WITHOUT A FIGHT

Following the terrorist group al-Qaeda's attack on the World Trade Center on September 11, 2001, the United States launched an offensive in Afghanistan to destroy al-Qaeda's bases in the country and topple the extremist Taliban regime (which harbored al-Qaeda's leader, Osama bin Laden).

In an operation code-named Enduring Freedom, U.S. aerial technology proved irresistible against a poorly armed adversary. The Americans enlisted the assistance of a ragtag anti-Taliban force called the Northern Alliance, made up Tajiks, Uzbeks, and Hazari Shias, providing special forces advisers and air support to help them capture the Afghan city of Mazar-i-Sharif on November 9.

Northern Alliance members then rushed south to attack the capital Kabul, the Taliban and its allies—Arabs, Pakistanis, and Chechens—flooding into the city to defend it. But U.S. aircraft bombed their positions relentlessly, which meant that when the Northern Alliance and its U.S. allies rolled into Kabul on November 13, they found it undefended.

1965

FIRST CLASH BETWEEN U.S. TROOPS AND THE N.V.A. AT IA DRANG

On November 14, 430 men of the U.S. 1st Battalion 7th Cavalry made a helicopter assault on what appeared to be an unoccupied landing zone in the Ia Drang Valley, in the Central Highlands of South Vietnam, only to come under fire from the North Vietnamese Army's (N.V.A.'s) 2,000-man 66th Regiment. The Battle of Ia Drang had begun.

The battle raged all day on the 14th and into the night. The next day, the 2nd Battalion joined their comrades in the fight against the N.V.A. U.S. air strikes and artillery fire prevented the U.S. soldiers from being overwhelmed, and on the morning of November 16 the air cavalrymen were withdrawn. U.S. losses at Ia Drang were 200 casualties. N.V.A. losses are unknown.

ALSO ON THIS DAY

1812

The two-day Battle of Smoliani comes to an end. The Russians defeat a demoralized French army suffering from frostbite.

1315

A VICTORY ON THE ROAD TO SWISS INDEPENDENCE

During the medieval period, the Swiss established their reputation as formidable warriors, especially when fighting on home soil. In 1315, for example, Archduke Leopold of Austria marched into Switzerland at the head of an army of 15,000 knights and foot soldiers. Having only 1,500 foot soldiers of their own, the Swiss sprang an ambush on the enemy at Morgarten, a narrow pass by the side of Lake Aegeri, in the foothills of the Alps.

The Swiss rolled boulders and tree trunks down the slope and then rushed down to attack the knights at the head of the Austrian column, driving the horsemen back into their own foot soldiers. The Swiss, in a tight phalanx, then cut down everything in their path, the Austrians losing 1,500 men.

ALSO ON THIS DAY

655

King Penda of Mercia's pagan army is defeated by King Oswiu of Bernicia's Christian army at the Battle of the Winwaed in northern England.

NOVEMBER 16

1632

DEATH OF GUSTAVUS ADOLPHUS AT THE BATTLE OF LÜTZEN

The Swedish King Gustavus Adolphus became the leading general of the Thirty Years' War, his aggressive tactics winning two notable victories, at Breitenfeld in 1631 and Lützen in 1632. He introduced a number of tactical innovations that included shorter pikes, lighter muskets, pre-packed paper cartridges, and lighter cannon to increase overall mobility and firepower.

When the Imperialist general Albrecht von Wallenstein marched into Saxony, Gustavus followed, the two clashing at Lützen, 15 miles (24 km) southwest of Leipzig. Both armies deployed in the usual fashion, with cavalry on the wings and infantry in the center, each force numbering 19,000 men.

Gustavus began the battle by assaulting the Imperialist Army. His cavalry on the right were triumphant but his infantry in the center were unable to drive back the Imperialist pikemen and musketeers. Gustavus was shot three times and killed, whereupon the Swedes were roused to fury and drove the Imperialists from the field. Wallenstein abandoned his artillery and withdrew under cover of darkness, 3,000 of his men dead on the field of battle. The Swedes had losses of 1,500 men killed and had secured their control of Saxony. But the death of Gustavus was a huge loss to the Protestant cause.

▼ A painting by Wilhelm Carl Räuber showing King Gustavus Adolphus praying before the Battle of Lützen.

1885

BALKAN BLOODLETTING AT SLIVNITSA

Having thrown off the Ottoman yoke, the newly independent nations in the Balkans soon began squabbling among themselves, chiefly over land. Serbia, seeking more territory, declared war on Bulgaria on November 14, 1885. The Serb king, Milan I, invaded Bulgaria with 25,000 men, the Bulgarian Army of 32,000 men, commanded by Prince Alexander, engaging the Serbs at Slivnitsa, 19 miles (30 km) northwest of Sofia.

On November 17, Prince Alexander made a spoiling attack to check the Serb advance, defeating subsequent Serbian attacks on November 18 and 19. Milan's troops were repulsed so thoroughly that they retreated in disarray, pursued by the Bulgarians.

ALSO ON THIS DAY

1796

The desperate three-day battle of Arcola, between French and Austrian troops in northern Italy, ends, with France's general, Napoleon Bonaparte, emerging victorious after narrowly avoiding death.

1803

LAST BATTLE OF THE HAITIAN REVOLUTION

The fight for freedom by Haitian slaves and former slaves lasted for almost a decade before they won their independence from France at the Battle of Vertières, fought on November 18.

The so-called Indigenous Army, 27,000-strong, under Jean-Jacques Dessalines and François Capois, marched to the Cape, the last French stronghold on the island, defended by General Rochambeau with 5,000 men. The brigades of the Indigenous Army stormed Fort Vertières, defeating a desperate French counterattack. Then a violent thunderstorm drenched the battlefield, after which Rochambeau withdrew. The next day he sent a courier to Dessalines requesting a cessation of hostilities. Haiti had won its freedom.

ALSO ON THIS DAY

1943

The beginning of a series of Royal Air Force Bomber Command attacks against Berlin in World War II. On November 18, 440 Lancaster bombers hit the city, causing minimal damage.

BRITISH DEBACLE AT BIR EL GUBI

During World War II, Italian soldiers and their equipment were often viewed as second-rate when compared to those of their German allies and their British and American enemies. It is certainly true that Italian units were often poorly led and were inadequately armed and supplied. Nevertheless, when deployed correctly and commanded intelligently, they were just as good as any other soldiers in uniform during that conflict.

In November 1941, during the war in North Africa, the British 8th Army, commanded by Lieutenant-General Cunningham, launched an operation, code-named Crusader, to relieve the besieged port of Tobruk in Libya. Axis forces opposing the British were the German Africa Corps and three Italian divisions, one of which, the Ariete Armored Division, which was dug in at Bir el Gubi, located around a crossroads. The unit tasked with destroying the Italian division was the British 22nd Armored Brigade, equipped with A15 Crusader tanks.

On November 19, the tanks of the 22nd Armored Brigade attacked the Italians at Bir el Gubi, the Ariete's anti-tank guns soon "brewing up" a number of Crusader tanks. In addition, the M13/40 tanks of the Italian divisions launched a counterattack that forced the British tanks to retire. At the end of the day, 57 British tanks lay burning after the Battle of Bir el Gubi; the Italians had lost 49 tanks.

Italian soldiers and their equipment were often viewed as second-rate when compared to those of their German allies and their British and American enemies.

▼ Italian tanks at Bir el Gubi.

1917

BRITISH OFFENSIVE STARTS
Beginning of the British offensive at Cambrai on the Western Front in World War I that marked the first large-scale, effective use of tanks in battle.

1759

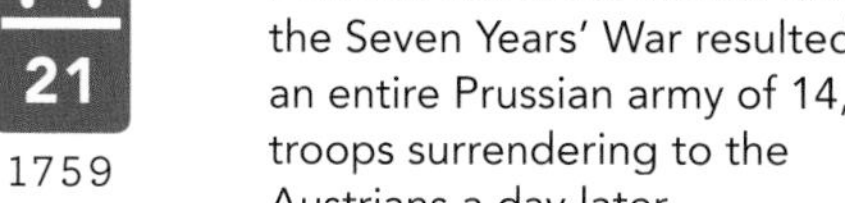

PRUSSIAN SURRENDER
Prussian defeat at Maxen during the Seven Years' War resulted in an entire Prussian army of 14,000 troops surrendering to the Austrians a day later.

1915

BRITISH TROOPS MAULED
British troops in modern-day Iraq were mauled by Ottoman forces defending the ruins of Ctesiphon, part of the forward defenses of Baghdad.

1808

SPANISH ARE OVERWHELMED
French victory at Tudela during Napoleon's campaign in Spain. Marshal Lannes overwhelmed a Spanish army commanded by General Francisco Castaños.

1542

KING JAMES V IS HUMILIATED
An English army defeated a Scottish force six times larger at Solway Moss in the Scottish Borders. The Scottish king died weeks later.

1863

FIGHT FOR THE RAILWAY
Start of a three-day battle in the American Civil War, in which Union forces in Tennessee secured a vital railway junction at Chattanooga.

1161

LIANG'S TROOPS MURDER HIM
The Song Chinese defeated an invasion by Emperor Wanyan Liang at Caishi on the Yangtze River. Later, Liang's troops murdered him in his tent.

1237

CRUSHING THE LOMBARD LEAGUE AT CORTENUOVA

The clash between the Italian states and the emperors of the Holy Roman Empire dominated the late Middle Ages in Europe. The Italian domains wished for greater autonomy, a desire that was vigorously opposed by the emperors.

Thus, when the Lombard League, an association of northern Italian towns and cities pressing for independence from imperial rule, raised an army to defend its claims, Emperor Frederick II marched south to crush it. The two forces met by a river crossing at Cortenuova in Lombardy, northern Italy. Unable to withstand the charge of the Imperial knights, the Lombard Army was all but annihilated.

The Italian domains wished for greater autonomy, a desire that was vigorously opposed by the emperors.

1803

VICTORY FOR WELLESLEY IN THE WAR AGAINST MARATHA

After his victory at Assaye, Arthur Wellesley, later Duke of Wellington, marched against the Rajah of Berar, fighting on November 28 near the village of Argaon.

The Maratha artillery was a force to be reckoned with, and within a short space of time it had inflicted casualties on Wellesley's infantry, causing three battalions to panic and flee. He managed to rally his men and launch a second assault, which broke the Maratha line at bayonet point. The defeated Maratha Army retreated to the fort at Gawilghur, which was captured soon afterward, but the war would go on for another two years.

ALSO ON THIS DAY

1899

During the Boer War, a British column attempting to relieve the besieged town of Kimberely fights a Boer force at the Battle of Modder River, Cape Colony, forcing the Boers to retreat.

1864

CONTROVERSIAL NON-FIGHTING EVENT OF THE AMERICAN CIVIL WAR

The Battle of Spring Hill, fought on November 29 in Maury County, Tennessee, was more significant for what did not happen than what did.

During the evening of November 28, General John Bell Hood's Confederate Army of Tennessee (12,000 men engaged) marched toward Spring Hill to cut the supply line of General John M. Schofield's Union Army (7,000 men engaged) as it withdrew toward Nashville. On the 29th, Hood's infantry converged on Spring Hill, which was defended by two reinforced Union brigades guarding the supply train. The Confederate attacks were beaten off, and they also failed to dislodge Union troops from the Columbia pike (the route north to Nashville).

As evening fell, Schofield's troops marched unmolested through Spring Hill to Franklin, passing by Confederate troops encamped for the night only a few hundred yards away. Hood therefore missed a golden opportunity to destroy Schofield's army on the march. This was unfortunate to say the least, as he would be defeated by Schofield the following day at the Battle of Franklin. The Battle of Spring Hill cost Hood 500 casualties to Schofield's 350.

1700

A BLIZZARD OF SWEDES AT NARVA

The Great Northern War began in 1700, Charles XII of Sweden defending his kingdom from the aggression of Poland, Denmark, and Russia. Peter the Great ruled the latter and, thinking the Swedes would be easily overrun, led an army of 40,000 troops to besiege the town of Narva, near the Gulf of Finland. But he had underestimated the restless genius of the young Swedish king.

Charles, 19 years of age, reacted immediately, landing an army of 10,000 troops near Narva and attacking the Russian siege lines at the Battle of Narva fought on November 30. A blizzard was blowing at the time, and Charles used the driving snow as cover for his greatly outnumbered force, attacking the Russian outposts before they could reply. Deploying his cavalry in large wedge-shaped formations, he crashed into the Russian Army, resulting in total confusion and panic among Peter's troops. After three hours of fighting the Russians fled, leaving a reported 10,000 dead on the battlefield. Charles' losses were barely 1,000 men.

With Narva recovered, Charles marched south to relieve Riga, which had been besieged by the Saxons, forcing the latter to withdraw in June 1701.

▼ A painting of the Battle of Narva.

CHAPTER
12
December

1914

THE BATTLE THAT SAVED THE AUSTRO-HUNGARIAN EMPIRE

On the eve of World War I, the Austro-Hungarian Empire appeared a formidable member of the Central Powers. But its officer corps was wedded to outmoded tactics, its troops were often ill trained, and the army's weapons and equipment were outdated. When war broke out in August 1914, Austria found itself hard pressed by the Russians.

In December 1914, around the towns of Łapanów and Limanowa in Galicia (now in southern Poland), a victory by Archduke Josef Ferdinand of Austria's 3rd and 4th armies saved Austria–Hungary from disaster. The Battle of Limanowa, which began on December 1 in Galicia, was the last engagement of the war in which the Austro-Hungarian Army achieved a victory against the Russian Army without the assistance of the Germans (albeit with the support of a single German division). The Austrian troops, exploiting a weak spot in the boundary line between the Russian 3rd and 8th Armies, promptly threw the Russians back. Russian plans for both a drive south of Kraków and an attack through the Carpathians were halted.

Both Russian armies were forced to retreat. The 8th Army had around 30,000 dead, wounded, or captured men. Austrian losses were 12,000 dead, wounded, or captured.

▲ Hungarian troops on horseback at the Battle of Limanowa–Łapanów.

1805

NAPOLEON'S GREATEST VICTORY

Napoleon's 1805 campaign established him as one of history's great commanders. Having led his Grande Armée east to deal with the massing forces of the Third Coalition of Austria and Russia, he staged a battle with the Austrian emperor and Russian tsar near Austerlitz, Moravia.

Tsar Alexander I and Emperor Francis II were confident of victory, even more so when they occupied the dominant Pratzen Heights before the battle. They mustered a combined total of 85,400 men, compared to Napoleon's 66,800.

The Battle of Austerlitz began when a large Austro-Prussian column advanced from the Pratzen to encircle the French right wing, another force advancing against the French left. Success seemed certain, but the arrival of Marshal Davout's III Corps and his reserve halted the Allied left wing, while V Corps and Marshal Murat's cavalry did the same to the Allied right wing.

Napoleon sent Marshal Soult's IV Corps to seize the now-empty Pratzen Heights, which were taken by midday, shattering the Allied center. Success became triumph when Napoleon wheeled the troops on the Pratzen right to surround what was left of the Allied right wing. The emperor and tsar fled, leaving 26,000 dead and wounded and 180 cannon on the battlefield. The Third Coalition collapsed soon after.

1800

AUSTRIAN DEFEAT AT HOHENLINDEN

The armies of the Napoleonic Wars all fought with similar weapons, such as the smoothbore muskets of the infantry, but in the realms of tactics and leadership the French were far superior to their rivals. The French Revolutionaries and then Napoleon encouraged initiative in their subordinates and promoted able men regardless of their social rank.

Thus, the commander of the French Army of the Rhine, Jean Moreau, was the son of a lawyer, but he was a gifted general who inflicted a heavy defeat on the Austrians at the Battle of Hohenlinden, fought on December 3, 20 miles (32 km) east of Munich. The Austrians suffered 4,600 dead and wounded, plus 8,950 captured, for French losses of 2,500 dead and wounded.

In the realms of tactics and leadership the French were far superior to their rivals.

THE U.S. AIR FORCE SAVES THE NORTHERN ALLIANCE

During the U.S.-led invasion of Afghanistan in 2001, the majority of the ground forces fighting the Taliban was composed of Hamid Karzai's Northern Alliance. But the insurgents were supported by U.S. combat aircraft flying round-the-clock missions to provide a 24-hour, 7-days-a-week air umbrella. The aircraft were directed to their targets by U.S. ground personnel accompanying the Northern Alliance, from units such as the 23rd Special Tactics Squadron.

At the Battle of Sayyd Alma Kalay, fought on December 4, Taliban forces launched a counterattack across the Arghendab River to throw back the Northern Alliance. But on the ground, U.S. Staff Sergeant Alan T. Yoshida single-handedly directed U.S. air strikes against the Taliban for eight hours, despite being under intense machine-gun and rocket fire. His accurate plotting ensured that the Taliban withdrew, at least 300 guerrillas being killed during the air strikes.

▼ Northern Alliance soldiers watch as U.S. air strikes pound Taliban positions in Kunduz province, Afghanistan.

1757

LEUTHEN: A TRIUMPH OF DECEPTION AND SURPRISE

When Frederick the Great engaged an Austrian army of 70,000 men under Prince Charles of Lorraine with only 36,000 troops, the odds were stacked against him. But the wily Prussian used deception to pin the Austrian right wing in the north with a small force, while rushing the main body of his army behind ridges to arrive at the Austrians' left wing in the south. Charles was forced to try to re-form his army to face south.

The Austrian cavalry on the right charged, to be thrown back by artillery and musket fire. The Austrian army then broke when charged by Prussian cavalry, Charles retiring after suffering 21,000 casualties. Frederick had suffered 6,400 casualties but was now the master of Silesia.

▼ Frederick the Great before the Battle of Leuthen.

CALIFORNIO LANCERS DEFEAT THE ARMY OF THE WEST

During the Mexican–American War of 1846–48, a minor battle lasting around 15 minutes took place at San Pasqual in San Diego County, California. A 100-man American mounted force, the remnants of the Army of the West, commanded by General Stephen W. Kearny, fought a force of mounted Californios, commanded by Major Andrés Pico.

Kearny had sent most of his men back to Santa Fe upon hearing the false information that California was in American hands. He was disabused of that notion when his men rode over the hills between Santa Maria and San Pasqual to encounter the Californio lancers in the valley below. Pico's men soon put the Americans to flight, killing 18 during the battle for the loss of 17 wounded.

A minor battle lasting around 15 minutes took place at San Pasqual in San Diego County, California.

▶ Brigadier General Stephen W. Kearny had captured Santa Fe, New Mexico, earlier that year.

THE SURPRISE JAPANESE ATTACK THAT BROUGHT THE UNITED STATES INTO WORLD WAR II

By late 1941, the Japanese had established a large empire in the Far East, and to expand it they decided to cripple the U.S. Pacific Fleet, based at Pearl Harbor, Hawaii, with a surprise attack.

The Japanese tried to expand their large empire by crippling the U.S. Pacific Fleet, based at Pearl Harbor.

Commanded by Vice Admiral Chuichi Nagumo, the attacking force was grouped into carrier divisions, each with its own air group. Division 1 comprised the carriers *Akagi* and *Kaga*, Division 2 *Hiryu* and *Soryu*, and Division 5 *Zuikaku* and *Shokaku*. Each carrier group had a complement of 21 A6M Zero fighters, 18 D3A Val dive-bombers and 27 B5N Kate torpedo-bombers.

The 213 aircraft of the first wave took off at 06:00 hours on December 7. An hour after the first wave had been launched, the second wave took off from the carriers: 50 Kates, 40 Zeroes, and 80 Vals. By this time, the first wave was approaching the target.

The battleships *West Virginia*, *Arizona*, *Nevada*, *Oklahoma*, and *California* and a target ship, the *Utah*, were all hit. All began to sink except the *Nevada*, which tried to steam out of the harbor. The battleship *Pennsylvania*, in dry dock, was also hit.

By 10:00 hours the aircraft were returning to their carriers, leaving five battleships and three destroyers sunk or sinking, three battleships and two cruisers damaged, and 3,478 military personnel killed or wounded.

◀ Japanese attack on the U.S. naval base at Pearl Harbor.

ALSO ON THIS DAY

1837

Canadian rebels are crushed by British troops and local militia at the Battle of Montgomery's Tavern, Toronto, during the Upper Canada Rebellion.

WHITE STORM, RED DEFEAT AT SUOMUSSALMI

The Winter War between the Soviet Union and Finland was a shock for the Red Army, whose ill-trained and poorly equipped troops came to grief against highly motivated Finnish troops who knew how to make use of the terrain and weather conditions.

By the end of 1939, the Red Army was ready to unleash its 44th Motorized Rifle Division and 163rd Rifle Division—48,000 men, 335 artillery pieces, and ten tanks—to link up at Suomussalmi and then drive west to Oulu, thus cutting Finland in half.

The Battle of Suomussalmi, which began on December 8, started with the Finnish 9th Division attacking the Soviet 163rd Division, first cutting its supply line and then placing a blocking force to prevent it from being relieved. The 44th Division tried to relieve the 163rd on December 25, without success. On December 30, the 163rd Division attempted to escape the trap at Suomussalmi, only to be cut to pieces by ski troops of the 9th Division and Finnish aircraft.

The Soviet 44th Division, meanwhile, was slowly ground down by Finnish sniper assaults, and by January 9, 1940, had ceased to exist as a fighting unit. The Battle of Suomussalmi cost the Red Army 22,500 men killed and wounded and ended the Soviet threat in central Finland.

▲ Finnish leaders gather to discuss their strategy after the Battle of Suomussalmi.

1824

PATRIOT VICTORY The Patriot victory over the Spanish at Ayacucho, Peru, resulted in the Spanish withdrawing their troops from the country, thus ensuring the independence of Peru.

1941

BATTLESHIPS SUNK The battleship *Prince of Wales* and battlecruiser *Repulse* were sunk by Japanese aircraft near Malaya, heralding the supremacy of naval air power.

1282

GRUFFUDD KILLED The Welsh leader, Llywelyn ap Gruffudd, was killed in battle at Orewin Bridge during Edward I's conquest of Wales. His head was displayed in London.

627

CIVIL WAR SPARKED Byzantine victory over the Sassanids of Persia at Nineveh, Mesopotamia, sparked a civil war in the Sassanid Empire and restored ancient boundaries.

1862

UNION ATTACKS REPULSED During the American Civil War, Union troops launched mass assaults against Confederate positions on Marye's Heights, Fredericksburg, Virginia.

1863

LAST BATTLE OF KNOXVILLE CAMPAIGN Confederate victory at Bean's Station, Tennessee, during the American Civil War, being the final battle of General Longstreet's campaign.

1864

NASHVILLE BATTLE STARTS The two-day battle at Nashville during the American Civil War destroyed Confederate General John Hood's army, which had invaded Tennessee.

1838

BATTLE OF THE BLOOD RIVER

Following the Great Trek of 10,000 Boers from Cape Colony to the north and east of the Orange River, South Africa, in 1838, the newly arrived immigrants to Natal came into conflict with indigenous Zulu tribesmen. The Zulus killed the Boer leader Piet Retief and destroyed the coastal settlement of Durban.

On December 16, the Boers made a stand along the Blood River, their muskets and wagon defenses repulsing attacks by around 10,000 Zulus led by the Zulu king Dingaan. By the end of the Battle of Blood River, around 3,000 Zulus had been killed. The Boers went on to found the Natal Republic.

The newly arrived immigrants to Natal came into conflict with indigenous Zulu tribesmen.

1812

VICTORY OVER NATIVE AMERICANS DURING THE WAR OF 1812

The war between Britain and the United States also involved Native Americans, who were often used cynically as pawns by both sides.

In Indiana, for example, Governor William Henry Harrison led a surprise attack by U.S. troops and militiamen on several pro-British Indian villages along the Mississinewa River. On December 17, the two-day battle of Mississinewa began with Harrison attacking four Indian villages and then destroying three more. The next day the Americans were attacked by 300 natives, the Federal troops repulsing them with musket fire. Over the two days the Indians lost around 45 warriors killed and dozens more wounded, and Harrison had eliminated any resistance in the Mississinewa River region.

The battle began with Harrison attacking four Indian villages and then destroying three more.

1745

THE LAST JACOBITE BATTLE FOUGHT ON ENGLISH SOIL

During the Jacobite Rebellion of 1745, the Scottish army of Prince Charles Edward Stuart advanced as far south as Derby, but retreated when the expected support from English Stuart sympathizers failed to materialize. Falling back north, it was followed by the English army of the Duke of Cumberland.

On December 18, the rearguard of the Scottish army and 200 of Cumberland's dragoons clashed at the Battle of Clifton Moor, near Penrith, Westmorland. In a brief but fierce engagement, the Scots charged the English, throwing them back. Ten English dragoons were killed and four more wounded. The Jacobites lost 12 men.

ALSO ON THIS DAY

1916

The Battle of Verdun on the Western Front in World War I ends. The ten-month battle has cost the Germans and French a combined 70,000 casualties a month.

WHEN BOTH COMMANDERS WERE CAPTURED IN THE SAME BATTLE

The Battle of Dreux was the only major engagement of the French First War of Religion (1562–3). The Huguenot Army, around 12,000-strong, clashed with a Royalist force of 18,000 troops at Dreux, in north-central France. The Huguenot cavalry was at first triumphant, the right wing charging and capturing the Royalist commander, the Duke of Montmorency, while the left pushed back Swiss troops fighting for King Charles IX. When the Huguenot commander, the Prince of Condé, was captured, the Royalists appeared to be on the verge of crushing the Protestants. However, the Huguenots rallied to allow their army to withdraw from the field.

▼ The French First War of Religion, the Battle of Dreux, takes place.

1943

THE CANADIAN FIGHT FOR ORTONA

The Italian campaign during World War II was far from being the soft underbelly into the Third Reich that senior Allied commanders had believed prior to its start. It was a grim, costly campaign of attrition.

A prime example was the Battle of Ortona that started on December 20, in which troops of the 2nd Canadian Infantry Brigade attacked to seize the north Italian town from German paratroopers, who had laid mines and booby traps throughout the town. In fierce, hand-to-hand fighting, the Canadians slowly cleared Ortona of Germans, the Adriatic town being liberated on December 28, by which time the Canadians had suffered more than 2,600 Canadian dead.

▼ A Canadian soldier checks a German machine-gun nest following its capture at Ortona.

1845

COSTLY VICTORY AGAINST THE SIKHS

The British desire to conquer India, at first through the East India Company, led to conflict with several Indian states and princes. European troops invariably triumphed against poorly armed and trained Indian levies, but the Sikh Army was an exceptional force that gave a good account of itself during the Anglo-Sikh Wars.

The desire to conquer India led to conflict with several Indian states and princes.

One such army, commanded by Sardar Lal Sing, dug in around the village of Ferozeshah, Punjab, in December 1845, awaiting the attack of the British Army commanded by General Sir Hugh Gough. The Battle of Ferozeshah, which began on December 21, started badly for the British, Sikh artillery repulsing the first attack, with a second clearing only a part of the entrenchments before darkness fell.

The battle was resumed the next day, the appearance of a second Sikh army discomfiting the British, who nevertheless held firm against cavalry attacks and won the battle, though Gough lost a sixth of his army.

1914

THE BRITISH EXPEDITIONARY FORCE IS BATTERED

In December 1914, at the request of the French, the British Expeditionary Force (BEF) launched an offensive in Flanders to push the Germans north.

The Battle of Givenchy concluded on the 22nd, following three days of futile and costly attacks by the BEF. British and Commonwealth units, many suffering trench foot and chilled to the bone by freezing rain, took their initial objectives, only to be thrown back by German counterattacks supported by concentrated artillery fire.

When the Battle of Givenchy petered out, the BEF had suffered losses of 4,000 for no strategic gain—a pattern that was to be repeated many times on the Western Front during World War I.

ALSO ON THIS DAY

1941

Communist Yugoslav partisans are defeated by Serb and Muslim forces in the Battle of Sjenica, in modern-day Serbia, during World War II.

1916

FIRST VICTORY FOR THE IMPERIAL CAMEL CORPS

By the end of 1916, the British and Commonwealth Egypt Expeditionary Force (EEF) had pushed Turkish and German forces back east in the Sinai Peninsula. The Turks had fortified a number of positions to prevent the EEF from entering Palestine, one of them being the northern Sinai village of Magdhaba, which was attacked on December 23 by soldiers of Major General Harry Chauvel's ANZAC Mounted Division, which had the Imperial Camel Corps Brigade attached. The camel riders rode to the assembly points and then dismounted to attack the redoubts around the village. The infantry, supported by machine-gun and artillery fire, succeeded in overcoming the defenses, the Turkish garrison surrendering in the afternoon.

ALSO ON THIS DAY

1793

A French revolutionary army of 18,000 troops crushes a royalist force numbering 5,000 men at the Battle of Savenay in western France, during the War in the Vendée.

1737

DECLINE OF THE MOGUL EMPIRE

By the beginning of the 18th century, India's Mogul Empire was in decline, its demise accelerated by the steady advance of Maratha power into northern India, which culminated in the Battle of Bhopal.

The two armies were huge, the Moguls mustering 100,000 troops and the Marathas 80,000 to make this the largest pitched battle fought in India during the 18th century. The Marathas triumphed over a corrupt and demoralized Mogul army and became the dominant power in central India. Mogul power never recovered and the empire would cease to exist some 20 years after the defeat at Bhopal.

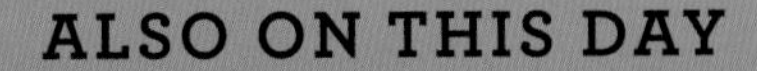

ALSO ON THIS DAY

1914

A German air raid on the port of Dover in World War I results in the first aerial bomb being dropped on British soil, creating a crater in a garden but causing no injuries.

1837

SWAMP BATTLE AT LAKE OKEECHOBEE

The Second Seminole War (1835–42) in Florida was caused by friction between white settlers and the indigenous Seminole who lived in the area. Colonel Zachary Taylor and 800 men cornered a group of Seminoles in swampy terrain near Lake Okeechobee. But the 400 warriors had prepared their defenses well and were armed with muskets.

When the Battle of Lake Okeechobee began on December 25, Taylor's men had to wade through thigh-deep mud to reach the Seminole positions, all the time being shot at by warriors behind log breastworks. After three hours of fighting, in which 26 of Taylor's men were killed and 112 wounded, the Seminoles jumped into their canoes and paddled off onto the lake, with 11 dead and 14 wounded.

ALSO ON THIS DAY

1941

The Battle of Hong Kong during World War II ends. Some 4,200 of the British and Commonwealth garrison of 12,000 is killed or wounded. The rest surrender to the Japanese after eight days of fighting.

1776

KEEPING THE FLAME OF AMERICAN FREEDOM ALIVE

By December 1776, the Revolutionary War was going badly for the Americans. George Washington had abandoned New York in November, crossing the Delaware River into Pennsylvania in December. The British Army went into winter quarters, expecting the new year to bring victory, but Washington had other ideas.

He devised a plan to cross the Delaware and attack the Hessian garrison at Trenton, New Jersey, to renew the revolutionary spirit. Despite the ice and a storm, his 2,400 soldiers made it across the river, reaching Trenton at daybreak.

Washington divided his force into two columns, one under Nathanael Greene attacking from the north, the other under John Sullivan assaulting from the west. The Hessian garrison—1,500 men under Colonel Johann Rall—was taken by surprise, the Americans quickly overwhelming the town in a running, one-sided firefight. Casualties on both sides were light—ten Americans killed and wounded; 105 Hessians killed and wounded—but almost the entire garrison threw down its weapons and surrendered.

The Battle of Trenton had been a remarkable American success, one that reinvigorated the patriot cause and demoralized the British.

1939

THE BATTLE OF KELJA UNDER SNOWFALL

During the Winter War between Finland and the Soviet Union, the Red Army continually tried to break through the Mannerheim Line, the defensive system on the Karelian Isthmus, the loss of which would leave the road to Helsinki open.

After several weeks of fruitless attacks in the Taipale sector, the Soviets switched their attempt to breach the Mannerheim Line to Kelja. The Red Army's 4th Rifle Division attacked across the frozen Lake Suvanto on the morning of December 25, 1939, under the cover of snowfall, to open the Battle of Kelja. The Finns were initially taken by surprise but recovered to blunt the Soviet attack with machine-gun and artillery fire. The battle ended on this day, a victorious Finnish report noting:

“The ice is littered with piles of bodies.”

▼ A Finnish Maxim M/09-21 machine gun nest during the Winter War, in area of the modern Pitkyarantsky District, Russia.

MARATHA VICTORY AT KOLHAPUR

The city of Kolhapur on the banks of the Panchganga River was the scene of a battle on this day between Maratha and Adilshahi forces, the latter having 10,000 troops to the Marathas' 3,500. But the Marathas were under the command of the famed warrior king Shivaji and included a high proportion of cavalry. Rustam Zaman's Adilshahi army included elephants, which were reportedly placed in the first line, even though they can be an unreliable battlefield asset, due to horses being nervous around them and their tendency to stampede in all directions if panicked. At Kolhapur, Shivaji attacked the enemy center and wings, putting them to flight. The ease with which he did so would suggest that the elephants did indeed stampede to create chaos.

▲ The Maratha Empire was founded by King Shivaji.

1503

THE TRIUMPH OF THE ARQUEBUS AT GARIGLIANO IN 1503

The Battle of Garigliano saw the French army of Louis XII defeated by a Spanish Army commanded by Gonzalo de Córdoba in southern Italy.

Córdoba had adapted the Spanish Army to incorporate new technologies, increasing the number of arquebusiers and preferring light cavalry to the heavy variety for such roles as scouting, screening, and harassing the enemy. He had been pursuing the French and took up a defensive position on the Garigliano River, opposite the French camp, with an old wooden bridge between them. He then had a pontoon bridge constructed a few miles upstream, which allowed him to get the main part of his army across the river and attack the French, who had been deployed to defend the wooden bridge. The surprise flank attack was entirely successful, in particular the firepower of the arquebusiers proving very effective against the dense phalanxes of Swiss pikemen in French service.

Of the 16,000 French troops that fought at Garigliano, some 4,000 were killed and a further 4,000 were either captured or fled. Spanish losses were 900. To add insult to injury, the Spanish also captured the French artillery train and baggage.

◀ French knight, Pierre Terrail, single-handedly defends the bridge at Garigliano, Italy.

1460

DEATH OF A YORKIST LEADER AT THE BATTLE OF WAKEFIELD

In December 1460, during the Wars of the Roses in England, Richard, Duke of York, was at Sandal Castle near Wakefield in Yorkshire, his forces gathering south of the stronghold. He had marched from London in response to a Lancastrian army mustering in the north around Margaret of Anjou, wife of King Henry VI. After Christmas Day, Margaret marched to Sandal Castle with 15,000 men to confront Richard.

Safe in his castle, it made no sense for Richard to fight the larger Lancastrian army (he had around 4,000 men), especially when reinforcements led by his son Edward were on the way from the Welsh Marches. But his sense of honor would not allow him to remain idle, so on December 30 he led his army out of the castle to attack the enemy.

The Lancastrians, initially taken by surprise, were forced back. But their greater numbers soon began to tell in a fierce contest. This would not necessarily have been decisive in itself, but Richard was wounded several times and lost control of his troops, which resulted in panic among the Yorkists. Rout soon followed and 2,900 Yorkists were cut down, Richard himself expiring during the battle.

870

WESSEX STANDS ALONE AGAINST THE VIKINGS

After they had conquered Northumbria, East Anglia, and Mercia, the Vikings turned their attention to the last remaining free Saxon realm in England: Wessex. The Norsemen had established a camp south of what is now the town of Reading in Berkshire, but in the 8th century was a rich Saxon estate. The Viking camp was situated between the Thames and Kennet rivers and was strongly fortified. Foraging parties were sent out on a regular basis, one encountering a Wessex force at the village of Englefield, between Windsor Forest and the Kennet River.

The Wessex men were under the command of Æthelwulf, Ealdorman of Berkshire (an *ealdorman* was a Saxon noble and royal governor of a shire, who commanded the *fyrd* [local militia] in times of war). In a short battle, the Vikings were routed, which suggests that the troops with Æthelwulf were his personal bodyguard and professional warriors, since the men of the *fyrd*—essentially civilians pressed into military service in response to an emergency—were far inferior when compared to seasoned Viking warriors. At least one Viking lord, called Sidric, was killed at the Battle of Engelfield, but there are no extant records of the losses suffered by each side.

INDEX

N

O

P

ACKNOWLEDGMENTS

As an author, one can say that many people and many things have been influences on one's writing. But for me, the person who first sparked my interest in history and military history in general, was my grandfather, Harry Darman.

Like many of his generation, he was man of few words and a stoic nature. A greengrocer by trade, he was caught up in the maelstrom of World War II, fighting in the British Army on D-Day and subsequently in Normandy and Germany in 1944–45. He witnessed not only the horrors of war but the obscenity of the Holocaust, being one of those who liberated Belsen. During my childhood, he only spoke of his wartime experiences in snippets, but they were enough to spark a young boy's interest in history and military affairs. That spark still burns.

Picture credits
The publisher would like to thank the following for the permission to reproduce copyright material.

Alamy
Chronicle: p11; INTERFOTO: p16; Everett Collection Inc: p19; INTERFOTO: p53; UtCon Collection: p55; Chronicle: p93; Science History Images: p113; GL Archive: p127; FLHC 3: p179; Everett Collection Historical: p180; Hum Images: p189; Chronicle: p199; Granger Historical Picture Archive: p203.

Getty Images
Corbis: p7; Bildagentur-online / Contributor: p13; Christian SIMONPIETRI/Sygma: p20; De Agostini / Biblioteca Ambrosiana: p25; Emmanuel Yevzerikhin/Slava Katamidze Collection: p30; Art Images/Heritage Images: p35; The Print Collector: p39; General Photographic Agency / Stringer: p41; DEA/ Biblioteca Ambrosiana: p43; Leemage/UIG: p47; Mondadori Portfolio: p59; Universal History Archive/UIG: p60; Archive Photos/ Stringer: p63; DEA / G. NIMATALLAH: p64; Universal History Archive: p67 Historical Picture Archive/ CORBIS/Corbis: p71; Arterra: p73; Universal History Archive: p75; Historica Graphica Collection/Heritage Images: p78; duncan1890: p82; ullstein bild: p83; Print Collector: p87; De Agostini Picture Library: p92; Topical Press Agency: p95; Hulton Archive: p97; Universal History Archive: p99; Hulton Archive: p103; Hulton Archive: p106; GraphicaArtis: p109; Universal Images Group: p110; Hulton Archive/ Stringer: p115; The Print Collector: p116; Sovfoto: p118; Interim Archives: p122; Universal History Archive: p123; Universal History Archive: p124; Hulton Archive/Stringer: p131; Universal History Archive: p133; DEA / BIBLIOTECA AMBROSIANA: p134; Keystone: p139; UUniversal History Archive: p140; Universal History Archive: p141; DEA Picture Library: p142; Buyenlarge: p146; clu: p149; Bob Thomas/ Popperfoto: p150; Corbis: p152; Hulton Archive / Stringer: p156; Universal History Archive/UIG: p158; Hulton Archive: The Galerie Bilderwelt: p161; DeAgostini: p165; Hulton Archive: p170; Genevieve Chauvel/ Sygma: p171; DeAgostini: p173; Heritage Images: p174; DEA Picture Library: p177; Photo12/UIG: p183; Imagno: p187; Hulton Archive/ Stringer: p192; Fine Art Images/ Heritage Images: p197; Patrick Robert - Corbis: p201; United Archives: p202; Bettmann: p204; Carl Mydans/The LIFE Picture Collection: p206; DEA / G. DAGLI ORTI: p209; Keystone/stringer: p210; Fox Photos/ Stringer: p214; Ipsumpix/Corbis: p215; The Print Collector: p216.

Shutterstock
Everett Art: p104; Sovfoto/Universal Images Group: p114; Granger: p146; Universal History Archive: p204.

Other
Creative commons: p51, p85, p90, p194; Crown copyright: p22; Public domain: p27, p29, p44, p79, p147/8 p168.

While every effort has been made to credit photographers and artists the publisher would like to apologise should there be any omissions or errors, and would be pleased to make appropriate corrections for future editions of the book.